Indomitable Spirit

By Kim Munro

Copyright

ISBN 978-0-9564435-0-2

Published by: Kim W. Munro
First edition
Fiction

About this book

This book is fictional. All characters and martial arts organizations mentioned in the book are fictional.

There is some adult content in this book. Parental guidance is recommended.

Terminology used in this book is contained in a glossary at the back of the book.

About the author:

Sensei Kim Munro holds the rank of Sandan in Shotokan karate-do and the rank of Shodan in Kenpo karate. She has trained in a wide variety of martial arts and kobudo all over the world. Kim lives just outside London, England where she runs a Shotokan karate club: www.pottersbarkarate.co.uk.

Cover artwork by Robert Verrill:

Robert Verrill is an artist and primary school teacher based in North London who also teaches art to children and adults at Insight School of Art. His creativity extends to projects as varied as designing stage sets for dance shows, illustrating poetry anthologies and running children's' art workshops in schools. He lives in North London with his wife and two sons. Contact familyverrill@aol.com

The Dojo Kun:

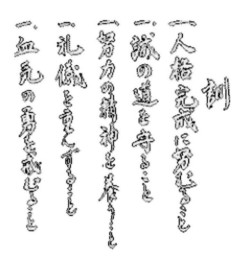

Strive for perfection of character.
Defend the paths of truth.
Foster the spirit of effort.
Honor the principles of etiquette.
Guard against impetuous courage.

Chapter 1
The remote mountains of northern Japan

'Again.'

Kayla's brain was telling her she couldn't get up again. Every muscle in her body hurt and her mind was saying 'Quit.' She thought back to the stern talk she'd been given by her master a few days back, about never giving up. Her master was testing her now, to see if she took that talk seriously and remembered the lesson. Kayla pulled herself up to her knees and gathered herself to face another opponent. As she stood, a fresh new sparring partner entered the dojo. She had already fought three hard rounds, each time with a new opponent that was not weary and bruised like she was now, from her previous rounds.

'Hajime', her master commanded the instant Kayla got to her feet again. Her master, who sat comfortably watching her student's every movement, showed no sign of mercy. No rest time between kumite rounds was given by the master. Kayla fought with all her might, out of necessity. Her opponent was coming in hard. After a minute had gone by, she found herself swept to the hard wooden floor once again. The sensei Kayla was sparring with was not satisfied with just sweeping her off her feet, and Kayla only narrowly avoided an axe kick coming down hard on her back by rolling out of the way, just in the nick of time. Kayla gracefully rolled back to her feet and carried on fighting, but her kicks were slow and labored now. She was weary, her next kick was caught by her sparring partner, and she was slammed back to the floor once again.

'Yame.' came from her master, and Kayla thought to herself 'thank god.' She had been thrown to the floor one to many times and had had enough now. Just as she was thinking this however, her master said 'Again.' Kayla rolled her eyes and groaned as she struggled to her feet once again. Her master held up her hand, signaling to the next sensei ready to spar with Kayla to stop entering the dojo, and said in a calm voice, 'Kayla, come over here.'

Kayla went over to her master and knelt down in front of her chair, 'Yes master.' she said, expecting to be praised for her valiant attempts to hold off four fresh opponents.

'Did you just roll your eyes at me when I said "again"?' Kayla grimaced, she was in trouble again. She thought to herself, it was impossible to please this master.

She answered, 'Yes master I did.'

Her master said calmly, 'Do you remember the talk we had the other day about never giving up and having an indomitable spirit?'

Kayla felt ashamed of herself, failing again, and looked down at the floor when she answered' 'Yes Master.'

Her master continued, 'Do you think rolling your eyes is acceptable etiquette in this dojo or with me?' Kayla could kick herself for her impetuous eye roll and groan; she should have just kept going until she was told she could stop.

'No master.' she answered still looking at the dojo floor.

'Do you think you are capable of learning the lesson of the indomitable spirit?' Master Harrington queried her student.

'Yes master, I do.' Kayla stated, hoping her master would not give up on her now.

'We will try again tomorrow then.' her master said. Kayla was both relieved her master had not given up on her yet, but also worried about doing this all over again tomorrow. 'Now, I want you to run the obstacle course ten times for rolling your eyes at me.'

Kayla knew if she reacted at all irritated or complained she'd be kicked out, so she just said 'Yes master', bowed, and got up off her knees to start her punishment.

As she started to walk away to the obstacle course her master said, 'take the stone with you.' Kayla thought, 'god, this woman was really pushing it'.

The obstacle course was hard. Ten laps of it was a pretty severe punishment, but adding the stone was another test to push Kayla to her limits. The stone was contained within a backpack and it weighed a good twenty pounds. It was difficult to do anything with it on your back. Kayla had worn the backpack with the stone before, when doing hundreds of kicks the last time she displeased her master. She knew how heavy it got after a little while with it on. She picked up the backpack that always sat near the entrance to Master Harrington's dojo, put it on over her gi and bowed as she left the dojo, headed for the outdoor obstacle course.

When Kayla crossed the finish line of the course for the tenth time, her once white gi was caked in mud and sweat. The final leg of the obstacle course required the runner to drop down on her belly and crawl under a series of low wooden planks. To add to Kayla's woes this afternoon, it was raining rather hard, and the crawl under the wood planks was a rather muddy affair. Kayla was covered from head to toe in mud and was pissed off by the time she finished the course for the last time. She took the stone off her back and sat down, catching her breath. She had barely been able to drag herself through the last lap of the slippery, water logged course. She was exhausted from her earlier rounds of kumite, the heavy stone on her back, not to mention the pounds of mud caked on her gi now.

'Do you listen to anything we tell you around here?' she heard from above her as she hung her head down between her knees catching her breath. Kayla was mad, what in the world had she done now?

She looked up and, still panting for breath said, 'Sensei, what have I done?' She felt like screaming, 'what the hell have I done wrong now!' she was so tired and fed up, but she knew better and kept her anger hidden.

He reminded her, 'How many times have we told you when you are out of breath you must stay standing and open your lungs, do not sit down and hang your head like that.'

Kayla rose immediately and opened her chest up by pulling her shoulders back as she had been told and panted, still struggling for breath, 'Sorry Sensei, I forgot.'

He looked a bit sorry for her and said, 'If you learnt your lessons well you would not feel as much pain.'

Kayla thought to herself 'Yes, he's right, I must start remembering what I am told and do it.' She replied to him 'Oss Sensei.' and bowed to him. He bowed back and walked on.

Chapter 2

The next morning, as Kayla knelt in front of her master, she was worried about what the day was going to bring. The opponents she had fought yesterday seemed like they were out to take her head off, coming in relentlessly and hard. Taking on a fresh kumite partner for each round was not an even playing field either. While Kayla grew more weary with each round, each new partner had the speed and stamina she lacked after several bouts. Her master's voice interrupted Kayla's thoughts, 'Kayla, are you ready for your challenges today?' Kayla wondered to herself if she should be truthful with her master and admit she was tired, bruised, and not really ready, or if she should just say 'yes' to show she was willing. She decided that she had better show some good spirit and said, 'Yes master, I am ready.'

Master Harrington sat looking at her student for a moment and then said, with the slightest irritation in her voice, 'Kayla, your mouth has told me you are ready, but I can see your spirit is not. You are just telling me what you think I want to hear, but you do not believe it yourself. You might endure today's challenges, to try to please me, but that is not the lesson of the indomitable spirit. Kayla, you are a talented martial artist, but your spirit holds you back.' Her master paused for a moment and sighed. Kayla wondered how her master could seemly read her mind; had Master Harrington heard her internal debate with herself? Had she heard her try to mentally psyche herself up to answer 'yes' with confidence? How had her master known her deep inner doubts? 'Kiritsu', Master Harrington commanded, and Kayla rose from seiza. 'Kayla, you are twenty-four years old and in your peak physical condition. I am an old woman. You should be able to easily defeat me, but you will not because your spirit is weak and mine has been trained and forged over the years to be strong.'

Her master stood up from her chair, took up a fighting stance and said, 'Come, attack me.' Kayla had never fought her master, or even seen her skills to any great extent. She was an old woman and Kayla knew she could beat her. Kayla launched a half hearted attack, not wanting to hurt the old woman she greatly respected. Kayla found herself on the hard floor quickly. 'Attack with spirit!' Master Harrington yelled, standing above her, waiting for her to get up again. Kayla was shocked; she had never heard her master raise her voice before. Although she'd been in trouble often enough with her, her master always kept a calm, quiet tone when speaking to her student. Now, Master Harrington's fierce tone was not a voice of anger, but of determination. She wanted to show her student real fighting spirit, and to see it reflected within her. Kayla thought to herself, 'ok, you asked for it.' and went in as hard as she could. Her master easily deflected all her attacks, seemingly without effort. As Kayla was getting tired, launching attack after attack, her master stepped in and swept her down on her back once again. This time, she followed it up with an arm lock across Kayla's throat that cut off her air. As Kayla lie on her back struggling for air, her master, with her arm still across her throat, said in an easy, gentle voice, 'Kayla, you leave this dojo today and think of the path you are going to take. If you can find your spirit, come back tomorrow. If you cannot, pack your bags and leave.' She released the lock across Kayla's throat leaving Kayla coughing and gasping for air on the floor. 'Get out of my dojo.' her master said as she turned her back and walked away from Kayla, and then added, 'Use this day wisely to find the spirit you will need to finish what you have started. If you set foot back in this dojo unprepared again, you will be sorry.'

Kayla flipped herself over onto her knees, bowed, and said, 'Oss master.' in a raspy voice, still struggling to recover from the arm lock across her throat.

Outside the dojo, Kayla sat on the steps and put her head in her hands. She was bitterly disappointed with herself. Kayla had never wanted anything else, for as long as she could remember, than to become a sensei for the WKIA. She had been dreaming and training for this for a long time, and now she was making a mess of everything and on the verge of being kicked out! Kayla got up from the dojo steps and walked down to the small mountain stream running below the dojo. As she sat on a rock watching the fast flowing stream rush by, she thought back to how it had all gone so wrong; she recalled her first week at the training camp.

Chapter 3
Months earlier

Kayla was so proud of herself. After years and years of training, and a previously rejected application, she had finally been accepted into the highly prestigious WKIA sensei training program. This was the hardest training program known in the martial arts world. Although it was rumored to be an exceedingly rough, there was actually very little known about it, other than it was tough. All who participated in the training camp were sworn to secrecy. Participants were not allowed to reveal where the program was held or any of the content of the training either. The only thing Kayla knew, from rumors, was that only about ten percent of the students who entered the program ever completed it, and only the top five students from each class were granted the coveted title of sensei in the WKIA. One hundred students entered the year long training camp. To be a sensei with the WKIA was to be amongst the best of the best martial artists in the world, and Kayla wanted that more than anything.

As Kayla walked along in the large group of martial artists trekking up a thin, steep mountain passage, she studied her fellow students. She wondered who amongst them would be the first to go and who would be in the top five. Everyone was different. There were tall and squat people, both men and women, shy and obnoxiously confident people, and people from many different countries from all over the world represented. Kayla knew enough from her experience never to judge a martial artist by their looks or by their talk. Sometimes the most confident talking person was actually the worst fighter, while the shy, retiring, tiny person could take anyone on. Kayla knew, until you faced someone in combat, never to pre-judge or underestimate their skills.

The group was trekking up one of the more remote mountain ranges in northern Japan to the secret training camp of the WKIA. They had all met at the Nartia International airport in Tokyo yesterday and then boarded a bullet train to transport them quickly up to northern Japan. From the train station, they were transported via several vans, up to the foothills of the mountains. The students were not told the exact location of the camp, nor could they exactly see where they had been driven to. The vans they were transported in were cargo vans rather than passenger vans and had no seats or windows in the back. The students sat on the van floor for the long, bumpy trip up to the foothills of the mountains. Kayla had been very relieved when they arrived at the starting point of the trek up the mountain to the WKIA training camp. The students carried everything they would need for the year, or however long they lasted, on their backs in backpacks. They were told they did not need much. In fact, they were given a list of what they could and could not bring. Five karate gis, running shoes, and toiletries was apparently everything they needed for the year! No electric equipment like iPods or blackberries were allowed. Kayla would have loved to take her blackberry with her, to communicate with her friends and family for the year she'd be away, but she supposed she'd learn to live without modern technology, music, and constant communication. They trekked up the mountain passage for nearly eight hours and just as the sun was setting, they arrived at the Shinto gates that marked the entrance to the camp. It was everything Kayla hoped it would be. The camp sat in a high mountain valley, surrounded by snow capped mountains. Ryokans, the traditional Japanese hostels, were dotted around a large old stone courtyard. A rocky, fast flowing mountain stream ran down along one side of the courtyard, and trees, now changing to there autumn hues were dotted all around. It was a beautiful camp and everything Kayla thought it would be.

Chapter 4

The ryokan rooms for the students were basic and not too comfortable for westerners unused to Japanese style accommodation. Kayla had always loved the idea of living simply and basically in a Japanese ryokan, however she quickly discovered they were not that comfortable of a place to live in. Kayla slid the shoji screen back and took a good look around what would be her home for, hopefully, the next year. The room was small and the floors were covered in tatami mats. In the corner of the room were rolled up futons, sleeping quilts, to be placed onto the tatami mat floor for sleeping. No pillows, mattresses, or extra blankets were visible in the small room. The rooms in the ryokan were separated only by thin sliding paper shoji screens. Kayla could already feel drafts of the cold night mountain air coming in under the thin screens. Noise travelled easily around the ryokan with only the shoji separating her room from the others. Although she could not see them, Kayla could hear her fellow students talking excitedly and unpacking, like they were standing right beside her. Two short, squat plain wooden tables sat next to the futons and a small wooden wardrobe sat at one end of the room.

As Kayla set her backpack down on the floor of her room, a Chinese girl slid back the shoji screen and entered Kayla's room. Kayla said, 'Hi. I think you're maybe in the wrong room.'

The girl flung her backpack against the wall and said abruptly, 'This is my room.' Kayla was surprised, she had thought this room was for her alone, but now realized she was to have a roommate in this small space!

'Are you in here too?' Kayla checked again. The Chinese girl looked tough and hard, she reminded Kayla of the girl gang members she'd dealt with a few years back. The girl just gave her the briefest nod and started getting her stuff out of her backpack and throwing it, unceremoniously, into the small wardrobe. Kayla introduced herself to the girl, who looked young to her, she guessed about eighteen or so. The unfriendly Chinese girl, her new roommate, was named Ling Mei, Ling for short. When Ling finished unpacking her backpack and Kayla went to unpack her things, she found Ling had taken all the space in the small wardrobe.

'This wardrobe is meant to be shared.' Kayla said to Ling, who had flopped down on the floor already looking bored.

Ling replied, 'You can use the floor.' meaning for Kayla to empty her things on the floor.

Kayla replied in a calm voice, 'I don't think so. Get up and move your stuff over to your half of the wardrobe.' Ling just sat starring at her and didn't move. Kayla was not about to be walked all over by this girl and took her arm and cleared the top shelf of the wardrobe of Ling's things with a sweep of her arm. Ling's stuff came crashing to the ground. As Kayla started to unpack her backpack, Ling leapt up from the floor and shoved Kayla hard, pushing her into the wardrobe. Kayla knew students could be kicked out for fighting so she turned and stuck out her hand and said, 'Let's start over again, my name is Kayla.' with a smile on her face.

Ling snarled, 'You pick up my stuff and put it back on the shelf.'

Kayla was not about to do that and replied back, 'Look, we have to live with each other for as long as you last here. So I suggest you start behaving like a civilized human being and not some street thug.' Kayla wondered how they let someone like this into the program. As Kayla stood starring at Ling, Ling sucker punched Kayla in the gut. Kayla doubled over with a groan, but came back up with an upper cut of her own that knocked Ling through the shoji screen.

Ling looked up at Kayla from the floor, the shoji screen in tatters, and yelled 'You bitch!' as she sprung back to her feet and launched an attack at Kayla. Kayla was deflecting her attacks when both girls stopped fighting immediately when they heard 'Yame!' in a booming voice from behind them. Stood in the hallway, looking at them through the torn shoji screen, was a large, squat, stern looking, Japanese man dressed in his white karate gi and a WKIA sensei's black belt around his waist. It was one of the WKIA sensei. Before either one of them could say anything, he said in a commanding voice, 'You two put your heavyweight gis on and be outside in two minutes or you can pack your bags and go home now!'

Kayla could not believe it; she'd been at the camp for no more than an hour and already she was making a bad impression and ready to be kicked out. She could kill this little troublemaker that was her roommate! The sensei started to walk away and said over his shoulder, 'Don't you dare speak or lay another finger on each other. I'll see you outside in two minutes!'

Even Ling looked a bit shell shocked by what had just happened; her tough exterior stripped away for a moment. Both girls changed quickly into their gis. Kayla put a white belt around her waist for the first time in years. All students, regardless of what ranks they had achieved in the outside world wore white belts at the WKIA training camp. Only WKIA sensei wore black belts and masters wore red belts at the training camp. Kayla held several black belts in different styles and was also a teacher, but here she was merely a student, a student in trouble now... she gulped.

The two young women stood at attention, side by side, in front of the sensei who had caught them fighting. Their gis were clean, neatly ironed, and stood out bright white in the dark night. It was about nine at night now, and the air was crisp and cold. Kayla could see her breath in the cold night air as she stood wondering how much trouble she was in now.

'Did I tell you to put your running shoes on?' the sensei said looking down at the girl's feet.

Kayla immediately replied, 'No Sensei' and started removing her shoes. Ling followed after her. As Kayla put her bare feet down on the cold stone slabs of the courtyard, she wondered how long it would be before her lips started to quiver in the cold. The girls stood at attention again after removing their shoes. The sensei circled around them slowly as he spoke. 'Did you two read the rules on the way here?' he queried.

Both girls shouted back 'Oss Sensei.'

He continued, 'So you know fighting outside the dojo is forbidden.'

The girls repeated 'Oss Sensei.'

He stood behind them for a moment in silence and then said, 'You can be kicked out for this offense.' Kayla gulped hard, but stayed in attention, eyes straight ahead. She felt like crying but did not. She was so mad at herself for getting into this situation. The sensei continued, 'Since you have not even begun your training here yet, I will give you one chance before I kick you out.' Kayla's toes were frozen now and she was having a hard time keeping her teeth from chattering, standing out in the dark cold mountain air, afraid to move a muscle in attention. 'Do you see that well over there?' the sensei pointed to a well not too far away from them.

'Oss Sensei' they answered in unison.

'Run over to it and fetch two buckets of water each from it. Next to the well you will find wooden yokes used to carry the water buckets across your shoulders. Come back to me when you've got the water buckets balanced across the yoke on your shoulders.'

Kayla and Ling said, 'Oss Sensei.' Kayla remembered to bow to him before she ran off to the well with Ling, while Ling did not.

Over at the well, the girls drew out four buckets of water from the well. The wooden yokes had notches at the ends of them to place the handles of the wooden buckets into. Kayla was amazed at how heavy the full water buckets were when she lifted the wooden yoke up and across her shoulders. She wondered how the much smaller and slighter Ling would manage such a heavy load, but the small Chinese girl was stronger than she looked, and Ling managed to lift the yoke across her shoulders. The whole process of getting the water out of the well, onto the yokes, and across her shoulders splashed the icy cold water all over Kayla. This made her already heavy gi wet and even heavier and her already cold body even colder. The two girls walked back to the sensei slowly, barefoot across the stone courtyard, with the heavy water yokes across their shoulders. Their arms were draped over the yokes to keep them balanced. Once back in front of him, he pointed to a building at the top of one of the valley's hills. It had wide stone stairs running up to it. 'You two make your way up and down those stairs to Master Morakami's dojo. If I hear you talking or I see you stop, you're out of here.'

Kayla bowed as best she could with the heavy water yoke across her shoulders and said 'Oss Sensei'. Ling just walked away toward the stairs.

About two hours into their stair climbing, Kayla was starting to get pretty tired. She was really fit, but no matter how fit one was, after hours with a wooden yoke on your shoulders, your back is going to start to ache. The stone stairs were very high. Each step up, from one stone to the next, required not only good balance with the water buckets, but also extremely strong upper leg muscles. Kayla was glad she had spent so many hours doing deep stance training to prepare for this program. Her upper leg muscles were strong. Kayla grimaced, little did she know she'd find her legs being tested like this the first night at camp! Ling also looked exhausted, but both girls kept going, wondering when the sensei, who had left them, would return to tell them they could stop.

Finally, the sensei reappeared at the bottom of the steps and said, 'Yame.' and the girls stopped in front of him again. Kayla was relieved this was over; she was tired and freezing cold, despite dripping in sweat from the effort. The sensei looked into their water buckets and said, 'Go fill those buckets again, they are almost empty.' Kayla was starting to wonder, already, if she could handle this place. Instead of coming out to stop their punishment, the sensei was only coming out to demand they add more weight back to their loads by filling up their water buckets again.

After a few hours more, Kayla saw the sensei come back out to the bottom of the stairs. When they reached the bottom once again, he said, 'Yame'. 'You may leave your water yokes and buckets back at the well and come back to me.'. Kayla was so relieved this punishment was over. She figured they had been out there for three or four hours now. The girls stood back at attention in front of the sensei again. They now looked a mess. Their once clean, white gis were now full of water and sweat and hung heavy off them now. Their hair, once pulled back tightly, now hung wild in their faces. 'What are your names.' the sensei demanded. The girls told them their names. 'No more fighting outside the dojo.' he paused and then said, 'You are dismissed. Bow in is at six a.m.' Kayla had the presence of mind to bow and say 'Thank you sensei.' while Ling turned and walked away with no bow, yet again. The sensei called her back, 'Ling, you show me no respect. Go fetch your yoke and water buckets and you continue your punishment.'

Kayla smiled to herself as she walked back to the ryokan by herself, watching Ling go to collect more water from the well. She thought to herself that she would have the room all to herself fairly shortly. Ling would not last long here, she was sure.

It was two a.m. when Kayla finally settled down on her futon in her room. She had cleaned up the mess they had made quietly, as all her fellow students at the ryokan were fast asleep now. Kayla also took the time to fix the wardrobe and fit both her and Ling's things into it, nice and neat. Kayla went to the shared bathroom to take a nice hot shower, and finally get warm. As Kayla walked into the bathroom for the first time, she was dismayed to see no showers. There were sinks, toilets, and in another room, she found a large cedar wood tub. She was very disappointed when she saw no tap into the tub, but only wooden buckets beside it. Apparently, one had to fetch the water from, probably the well outside, to have a bath. She groaned aloud. Kayla had to settle for a splash in the sink to clean herself up. And, the final blow for the evening, no hot water came from the sink taps! It was freezing cold, fresh mountain water. When she finally laid down on the futon in her room, although she was exhausted, she couldn't sleep. She couldn't turn her brain off. She was very upset she had been in trouble so soon, and made a very bad first impression with one of the sensei.

Kayla must have dozed a bit, because she awoke with a start when she heard a loud gong sound coming from the bottom of the ryokan. Kayla felt like she had just fallen asleep. She opened her eyes a slit and found it was still dark outside. She groaned, rolled over, and closed her eyes again until she started hearing her fellow students starting to get up and get ready. She fought with herself as she lay there, trying to convince herself to get out of bed. Only the thought of being in more trouble, for being late for morning bow in, and the uncomfortableness of her 'bed' on the hard floor made her finally get up.

Kayla put on a clean white gi. The one she had worn last night was still hanging wet over the wardrobe. With no heating in the room, she wondered how long it would take for the heavyweight gi to dry. This was not how she wanted to start her first morning at the training camp, both physically and mentally tired from her punishment the night before. Kayla wondered where Ling was as she dressed for bow in. Kayla found her breakfast and all her fellow students downstairs in the common room of the ryokan. Breakfast consisted of a large bowl of steaming white rice and a hot cup of lovely smelling tea. It was the first time she felt somewhat warm, eating and drinking the hot rice and tea. Kayla was ever so pleased to see, in the middle of the common room, a wood burning iron stove. The stove had a large kettle of boiling tea steaming away on top of it. She stood close to it to get warm. As the other residence of the ryokan all stood around the stove eating and drinking their breakfast, her fellow students quizzed her about what had happened between her and her roommate. Kayla was sure they had all heard the entire fight anyway, but it didn't stop them from prying. Kayla did not want to inflame the situation between her and Ling any further, so she didn't comment much, just saying, 'We had a small disagreement.' and left it at that. This comment invoked chuckles from her fellow students, some of whom had seen Ling smash through the shoji screen from Kayla's punch.

Chapter 5

As they left the ryokan to go into the central courtyard for morning bow in, everyone dressed in clean, white gis, Kayla felt inspired again at being here. It was a beautiful sight, the snow capped mountains all around them and one hundred martial artists all walking out into the stone courtyard, surrounded by lovely old wooden ryokans, the Shinto gate at the front, and the sun gently rising above the gates. As they walked out into the courtyard Kayla couldn't believe it when she saw Ling still walking up and down the stairs with the water buckets. Wow, she thought, that sensei must have really been pissed off with Ling's disrespect. Even she felt slightly sorry for Ling now. She also felt a bit of respect for the girl. She'd been walking up and down those steps for about seven hours! The students lined up in ten lines of ten in the stone courtyard in complete silence and in attention. Of course, one line was one person short, Ling. The sensei emerged from their ryokan and lined up in front of the students. The sensei who had caught Ling and Kayla fighting looked back at Ling heading down the stairs again and yelled to her, 'Come Ling, bow in with everyone.' Kayla thought to herself, 'you had better thank the sensei and bow or you're history girl' as she watched Ling head toward the sensei, looking completely disheveled, exhausted, and pissed off.

Ling apparently was capable of learning from her mistakes and bowed and said, 'Thank you sensei.' in a civil tone of voice.

'Seiza.' was called loud and clear and the students and sensei all knelt down on the hard stone slabs for bow in. Immediately after bow in the students were told to put their running shoes on and run up the mountain path that ran alongside the stream that flowed near the back of the ryokans. They were told there was a pagoda at the top of the path. They were to run to the pagoda, and back down. Kayla's legs were tired from the stairs she had climbed up and down for hours last night, but she drove herself on, now pumping with adrenalin. It was a long, steep uphill climb over rocks and roots and through overgrown areas of the path. No one had any idea how far away the pagoda was, but everyone was keen to be the first to get there and was running fast. When Kayla started to see runners coming back toward her, she realized, she must be near the pagoda. She was very happy to be half way done. Coming back down the mountain, however, proved to be just as difficult, if not more, than going up the path. More than a few runners lost their feet from underneath them on the way down, and found themselves sliding down the path on their bums.

Kayla and Ling were the last two students to come back into the courtyard from the morning run up the mountain. A sensei stood waiting for the student's return. He gave them each a number, out of one hundred, designating what place they finished in. As Kayla went past him she heard, 'Ninety-nine'. This upset Kayla, she knew she could do a lot better, if only she had not been exhausted from the start! Ling crossed quite a few minutes behind Kayla, 'One hundred.'

Kayla was amazed Ling finished the run at all after her night on the stairs. Ling fell to the ground as she passed the sensei. The sensei commanded calmly, but firmly, 'Get up.' looking down at Ling. Ling didn't get up. Kayla, who was standing near by, went to her roommate and helped her up. Ling's body was shaking and she had a look of pain on her face, but she managed to gasp, 'Thanks.' to Kayla. Kayla was unsure if the thanks was genuine or if she was being sarcastic.

At the end of the first day's training, the students again lined up in the courtyard to bow out with their sensei. As they completed bowing out, still sitting in seiza on the hard stones, one of the sensei announced, 'Each of you was given a number when you completed this morning's run to the mountain pagoda. Everyone with a number ninety or below is dismissed. The rest of you come with me.'

Kayla and Ling glanced over at each other. Ling didn't look like she could take much more, and Kayla was also feeling the strain. The ten students who had come in last during the morning run stood at attention in front of the sensei while the rest of the students headed back to their ryokans. 'The students that finish in the bottom ten on the morning run must clean the dojo floors at the end of the training day.' the sensei announced. 'You will find buckets and rags over at the well. Make sure those floors are spick and span.'

All ten students replied, 'Oss sensei', bowed, and trotted off to the well. There were ten separate dojos at the training camp and each student was given one to clean. Kayla's back and legs were already aching from carrying the water yokes last night and the long day's training sessions, but she figured it was almost over now. What she really wanted now was a mop, but only rags were provided. She figured it was either down on her hands and knees to scrub the floor or bend over and run up and down the wooden floor with the rag stretched out in front of her. Both options seemed unappealing to her sore legs. She decided running up and down the floors with the rag would be the faster option and started on her task. It took Kayla about forty-five minutes to clean the floor in her dojo. When she returned to the ryokan she was exhausted. Ling still wasn't back yet!

When Ling finally slid the shoji screen back and entered the room, she looked down at Kayla crashed out across the tatami mats with her dirty gi still on and said, 'Shit, that was one of the hardest days of my life.' as she collapsed on the floor next to Kayla. Kayla briefly wondered what other days of Ling's life compared in hardship to the one she just had. Kayla was tired, but managed to try to encourage her young roommate, 'I don't know how you stayed on your feet all day today. You have a lot of spirit.'

Ling groaned and mumbled, 'I can't afford to get kicked out of here.' and rolled over, turning her back on Kayla not wanting to talk anymore.

Chapter 6

Kayla looked with dismay into the empty wardrobe. All her karate gis were dirty. It was only the fifth day of training, but because she had used a gi the night she was punished for fighting, she was now out of clean gis one day before she should have been. She panicked; she couldn't turn up for bow in in a dirty gi! 'Shit' she said aloud.

Ling queried her roommate, 'What's up?' Kayla told her she was out of clean gis. Ling, because she had worn the same gi all night and right into the next day's training still had one clean gi left. 'Listen, since I got you in trouble the first day, I'll give you my last clean gi.'

Kayla couldn't believe the girl who had a tremendous chip on her shoulder, and seemed to hate her from the get go, was now being generous and offering to make amends for getting Kayla into trouble. Kayla queried, 'Are you sure?'

Ling replied, 'Not really, but I guess I owe you one.'

Kayla thought, 'ya you do owe me one.' but said aloud, 'Thank you.' and pulled Ling's clean gi out of the wardrobe. It was one size too small on Kayla, but it was better than turning up in a dirty gi Kayla thought. Ling put on the cleanest gi she should could find in the room, which wasn't that clean!

Ling stood out like a sore thumb at line up that morning in her dirty gi. The sensei that had punished her for fighting a few nights ago got right up in her face and said, 'Ling, did you not learn the lesson of respect the other night?'

Ling was not sure how to reply, she had learnt the lesson and meant no disrespect with her dirty gi. She was only repaying the small debt she felt she owed Kayla for starting the fight the other night. 'Oss Sensei.' she replied.

'Then why do you disrespect the sensei and your fellow students by turning up in a dirty gi, unprepared?'

Ling could only reply, 'Sorry Sensei.'

Kayla, who was standing at attention right next to Ling in line, couldn't stand it, she piped up, 'Sensei, it is my fault.'

The sensei moved in front of Kayla now, 'Why is it your fault?' Kayla briefly explained to him what had happened. The sensei paused for a moment before he said to both of them, 'Although I am heartened that you two have patched up your differences and apparently have become friends now, this still does not excuse you from coming to bow in in a dirty gi. You both report to me after training today.' Kayla and Ling both replied, 'Oss Sensei.' and glanced at each other, wondering what horrors awaited them after training today.

Both Kayla and Ling improved their performance on the morning run and were no longer in the bottom ten. After training today, however, they had to report to Sensei Komhara to see what their punishment would be for the dirty gi incident. He asked the girls to follow him, and he led them to the back of the sensei's ryokan. There were a pile of dirty gis out the back of the ryokan. 'You will wash and iron the sensei's gis. Also, go get your own gis so you do not find yourself in this situation again tomorrow.'

There was no modern equipment at the camp and the girls found washing and ironing about thirty gis was not only a lot of hard work, but also took a very long time. Water had to be fetched from the well in buckets and brought to a large wooden trough. Detergent was poured in, and stones at the bottom of the trough were used, with lots of hand labor, to pound the dirt and sweat out of the gis. The heavy, wet gis were then carried down to the stream to be rinsed out. Down at the stream Ling turned to Kayla and said, 'You should have kept your mouth shut this morning when Sensei Komhara was questioning me about the dirty gi.'

Kayla replied, 'I couldn't stand right next to you and listen to him accuse you of disrespecting him again. Something you were not guilty of... something that was my fault, or partially my fault anyway.'

Ling scoffed, 'You're real goodie-two-shoes aren't you?'

Kayla was starting to get pissed off with this kid again, 'If you call being truthful and trying to stick up for a friend a goodie-two-shoes then ya, I guess I am.' she paused and added, 'In my book, that's better than walking around with some big chip on your shoulder, angry at the world, and anyone who tries to be civil to you.'

The girls were quiet for a while, while they continued to rinse and ring out all the gis in the stream, realizing they were heading toward another fight if they carried on speaking to each other. Kayla tried to reach out to Ling once again, changing the subject, 'My hands are killing me. I'm starting to get blisters ringing out all these gis.'

Ling replied, 'Ya, me too.' It was starting to get dark as the girls were finishing up down at the stream, when Sensei Komhara approached them, 'Ok girls, you can take the gis over to that hut across the courtyard,' he pointed to it. 'There the gis can be dried and ironed. When you've ironed all the gis you are dismissed.'

The girls both bowed and said 'Oss sensei.' As they carried the gis across the courtyard Kayla said to Ling, 'I don't suppose there's going to be nice tumble driers and steam irons in there.'

Ling smiled a little and replied, 'Suppose not.'

As they entered the hut, Kayla was delighted by the warmth that hit her as they opened the door. She was really cold again, after washing all the gis out in the icy cold mountain stream. A fire blazed beneath hot glowing rocks. On top of the flat rocks were heavy irons heated by the rocks. Kayla turned to Ling, 'This is going to take forever!'

Ling was starting to warm to Kayla a bit now. She was impressed by this girl. Most people were scared of Ling, put off by her quick temper and somewhat brisk personality, but Kayla was not scared of her and was not giving up on her attempts to make friends. Ling dropped her guard a little, 'I guess we are going to miss dinner tonight. Do you think they'll feed us?'

Kayla replied, 'God, I hope so, I'm absolutely starving. But given we are probably not Sensei Konhara's favorite students right now, I'm not sure if he'll remember we have missed dinner.'

Ling replied, 'Ya, he's tough. I still can't believe he had me climbing those steps all night long!'

Kayla could see Ling was now making an effort to try to be friendly and talk with her and replied, 'Ya, I'm still amazed you managed to do it and train all day the next day!'

The girls spread the gis out around the hut to get them dry and began the task of ironing all of them. After a few hours Sensei Komhara kicked the swinging wood door open, walking through it with two plates in his hands. Both girls stopped and bowed 'Oss sensei.'

He bowed back to them and held out the dishes, 'Dinner.'

The girls replied, 'Thank you sensei.'

Over their dinner in the laundry hut Kayla asked Ling, 'So Ling, if we are to be roommates for the next year, why don't you tell me a bit about yourself.' Kayla caught, what she thought was a flash of panic in Ling's eyes, for just a moment, before Ling quickly looked down at her food to avoid Kayla's gaze. Ling shoved some food in her mouth giving her time to think for a moment before answering Kayla.

Ling replied, 'I grew up in China and have studied wushu, kung-fu mostly. My sifu taught me karate too, telling me it would make me a more well rounded martial artist, but karate was always second to kung-fu.'

Kayla waited for more to come from Ling, but apparently this was all she was going to get for now. Kayla replied, 'Wow, I've always wanted to go to China and study kung-fu.' trying to extract more from Ling.

Ling replied, 'We better get back to work or we'll still be ironing at morning bow in'. Kayla thought to herself 'well, this is a start... maybe over time this girl will open up a bit and relax.'

To break up the monotony of the ironing Kayla decided she'd tell Ling about herself. She'd given up on Ling ever asking her anything.
'I'm from Indiana, a state in the mid-west of the U.S. I've been training in karate since I was a little girl. My family, my mom, dad, and big brother all still live in Muncie, a small town in Indiana. I miss them a lot. It's really hard being here and not being able to communicate with them. I don't think I've ever gone for more than a month without talking to them.' Kayla wasn't sure what she saw in Ling's face now, was it jealousy, or did she just think Kayla was soft, wanting to talk to her family? Kayla asked Ling, 'Do you miss being able to talk to your family?'

Ling replied flatly, 'I don't have any family.'

Kayla replied, 'Oh, I'm sorry.' and wondered if she should ask what had happened to them or not. She realized by now that Ling was not going to quickly open up to her, but she tried, 'If you don't mind me asking, what happened to your family?'

Ling had that briskness back in her voice again. She was irritated with Kayla's probing questions, 'Mind your own god damn business.' she snapped back.

Kayla just said, 'Sorry.' and the girls fell silent again. As they were finishing up, ironing the last two gis Kayla thought she didn't want to leave their conversation the way they had, and bravely spoke again, 'Ling, I'm just guessing here, but I'm guessing you've had a hard life.' Ling stopped ironing and looked at Kayla, surprised this girl just never gave up trying to communicate with her. 'Look, I want us to be friends. I'm sorry if I pry too much. You clearly are a private person. Maybe over time you will come to trust me as a friend.'

Almost everyone Ling had ever trusted had let her down, with one exception, her kung-fu sifu, Sifu Suxi. Trust did not come easily to Ling, but she was starting to like Kayla and replied back to her, 'I'll try to be your friend, but I gotta warn ya, I'm a pretty lousy friend.'

Even though they were exhausted, both girls lie awake that night thinking. Kayla wondered what had happened to Ling's family and why she clearly didn't trust anyone and was so guarded. She wondered if friendship would be possible with this difficult girl. Ling wondered if she could trust Kayla. What she had seen of her so far told her she was quite capable of being a loyal, trustworthy friend. No one Ling knew in her past would have voluntarily stepped forward to defend her like Kayla had done when Sensei Komhara accused her of disrespecting him again. Kayla couldn't have known, when she told him it was her fault Ling was wearing a dirty gi, what the penalty would be. She could have been kicked out for lying or something. Ling still wasn't sure she wanted to trust anyone again, but Kayla was going to a difficult person to push away.

Chapter 7

That first week had been tough, and Kayla still cringed to herself as she recalled the horrible first impressions she'd made on the sensei that first week. As Kayla sat on the rock, starring into the stream, she thought to herself she couldn't fail now, she'd been through so much these past months. She had to find the spirit her master now demanded to see in her... somehow. Over the nine months she'd been at the camp, many students had dropped out or were asked to leave. But both Kayla and Ling were still there, fighting for their places in the top five. Kayla recalled the day the masters selected their students...

Chapter 8

The winter training was particularly hard for Kayla. She hated being cold and it was freezing up in the mountains during the winter months. Kayla was relieved when a few kerosene heaters had arrived at the ryokan to make the freezing cold floors almost bearable. Along with the heaters also arrived some extra futons. But despite the extra heaters and futons, Kayla often lay on the drafty floor and dream of a hot shower and a warm duvet and bed to jump into after a hard day's training. Well, she thought she was getting tougher, and she imagined that had to be part of the training. They didn't want sissies as sensei of the WKIA for god sake! If she was not strong enough to handle a winter in the mountains, she was not worthy of being a WKIA sensei.

The worst part of winter training was morning bow in. The ryokan floor always felt cold to Kayla, until she walked out the front door, in her bare feet, onto the ice and snow covered stones in the courtyard and stood at attention in the icy wind that whipped off the mountains across the open courtyard. The students and sensei still knelt in seiza and stayed out there for as long as they had when the temperatures were pleasant. The training sessions all took place in the slightly warmer dojos dotted around the camp, however bowing in and out and the many daily announcements all took place out in the icy, cold courtyard. Kayla learned over time, from watching her sensei, how to hide her pain. She steeled her eyes forward and tried to ignore the cold wind, which caused her more pain than any blow she'd taken thus far in training. She still felt the cold as badly as she had the on the first day, but she didn't show it on her face anymore. She bit her lip to stop her teeth from chattering, and even though she couldn't wait to get out of the freezing wind, she looked tough, and tried to look as if she could kneel there all day long if need be.

The mooring run up the mountain had also taken on a new level of difficulty as the students, still only in their running shoes, now ran through heavy snow drifts along the mountain trail. Sometimes the large pine trees above them let loose, dumping snow onto the runners that had disturbed them down below. The runners now came across the courtyard finish line with their gis completely soaking wet from the snow. Quite often Kayla found her gi had a thin layer of ice on it, when she dared to stop moving for too long.

'Kiritsu'. All the students rose from seiza and bowed out as an icy wind blasted across the courtyard and right down Kayla's spine. Kayla turned to Ling, walking beside her, back to their room in the ryokan, and said, her voice barely audible with bad laryngitis, 'I can't do this anymore, I'm quitting.' Kayla had been training for the past two days with a sore throat, laryngitis, a stuffed up nose, and the chills. On the run up the mountain this morning she had to stop several times and throw up along the way.

Ling replied, 'Come on, let's go back to the room and I'll get you a nice hot cup of tea and you'll feel better.'

Kayla was too tired to argue with her and just said, 'No, I've had enough.' and started to break away from Ling and walk toward the sensei's ryokan to quit. Ling grabbed her upper arm and dragged her back on the path to their room and said, 'I'm not letting you quit Kayla.' Kayla made a pathetic attempt to remove Ling's grip from her arm, but she was too weak with illness to fight with Ling.

Back in the room Kayla crashed onto the futon on the floor groaning. Ling came in a few minutes later with a steaming hot cup of tea, 'Come on, sit up and drink this.' she said looking down at Kayla. Kayla sat up and wrapped the futon around her shoulders and started sipping the hot tea. After a few sips she rasped again, 'I'm quitting.'

Ling put her futon on top of Kayla, who was shivering, giving her some more warmth. 'See how you feel in the morning before you make a rash decision.' Ling replied wisely. Kayla thought this was good advice and she didn't think she could get up from the floor again anyway!

The next morning Kayla still felt horrible and didn't get up when the gong signaled it was time to rise for breakfast. Ling let her sleep a while longer but then nudged her with her foot and said, 'Come on Kayla, you gotta get up for breakfast.'

Kayla rolled over and whispered, her voice still not working, 'I can't.'

Ling bent down and ripped the futon covering Kayla off her and yelled, 'Get the hell up!'

Kayla curled herself up shivering and rasp, 'Put that back on me.' meaning for Ling to put the futon back over her.

'Make me.' Ling challenged, standing above Kayla with her hands on her hips. Ling went to the wardrobe and pulled out a clean gi and threw it on top of Kayla, 'Get dressed.'

Kayla sat up and moaned, 'I can't do this.'

Ling replied, 'All you ever tell me is how much you want this and now you want to throw it all away because you're a little sick? - get on your feet!'

Kayla got up and threw her karate gi on. She didn't know how she'd make it through the day, but she'd give it another try.

As they bowed out later that afternoon, Kayla turned to Ling as they walked back to the room and said, 'Thanks friend.'

Ling smiled, 'What are friends for - to kick you ass when you need it', she laughed.

Kayla, still whispering said, 'And you told me you'd make a lousy friend.' and smiled. Kayla thought of Ling now as the little sister she had always wished she had. After an extremely rocky start, the girls had learnt to respect each other and now were looking after each other like friends should. Kayla was starting to appreciate Ling's sarcastic wit as Ling shot back 'I only stopped you from quitting cause I know I can kick your ass and make it into the top five even if you stick around.'

Kayla laughed and rasped back, 'We'll see about that.'

As the spring started to arrive, many of Kayla's fellow students had dropped out. Some because of the harsh conditions, some missing family too much, some that just couldn't take the hard pace of the training seven days a week, and a few, Kayla really felt sorry for, that sustained injuries and just couldn't go on. She worried about that. It was so easy to injure yourself during sparring, during the run up the mountain, doing anything really. Injuries were treated, but if the person couldn't carry on, they had to start all over again in next year's program, if they didn't want to drop out completely, which everyone Kayla knew that was injured did. She couldn't blame them, it was too difficult to start all over again.

One early spring morning, as they sat in seiza in the courtyard, a light rain steadily coming down on them, one of the sensei announced the masters would be arriving at the camp today. Kayla and her fellow students were surprised by this announcement. All of them had assumed the sensei were their teachers, and they would make the selection of students to be promoted. The students were informed there were ten masters and each master would select only one student to train. Students not selected would be cut from the program. Kayla did not need to look around and count, she knew exactly how many students were currently left. Out of the one hundred students that had begun the training six months ago, only twenty-six remained. Those were not good odds, Kayla thought to herself, ten out of twenty-six. The sensei continued to explain to the students that the masters would take advice from the sensei about the students' capabilities and would also observe the training for two weeks before decision day.

Kayla could feel the tension rise in the courtyard as the sensei spoke. Every student could feel the pressure they would be put under in the next two weeks, with every movement being watched by the masters. It was like starting all over again, with a new set of teachers now judging them.

Chapter 9

Dinner was always a formal affair at the camp. It was always at eight p.m. prompt. Students had to be fully cleaned up and dressed in the silk kimonos and trousers, issued to them on arrival, by ten minutes to eight. The students entered the dining hall first and stood at their assigned places along the long, low wooden tables that ran the length of the dining hall. The dining hall was plain and simple. At the front of the hall, there were a few steps and a raised floor area. A head table sat up in this area that ran perpendicular to the students' tables. This was where the sensei were seated. The sensei entered the dining hall after the students, went to the front, faced their students, and everyone bowed. Once the sensei were seated, kneeling at the front table, the students knelt on command by the chief sensei, 'Seiza.' The dinners were good and there was plenty of food. This was a good thing since rice and tea were the only things on offer during breakfast and the short lunch break. Kayla was by no means overweight, but even she had lost about ten pounds here, with the hard training and the only decent meal being dinner.

The students realized this evening's dinner would be different when they saw another table laid out parallel besides their tables. When the sensei came in this evening, they went to the front to bow with the students but then stood alongside the new table parallel with the students and waited in silence along with their students. When the doors opened again, everyone in the dining hall, standing in attention and silence, the masters entered the hall and went to the front. The chief sensei commanded, 'Master ni rei' and everyone bowed to the masters standing at the front of the hall. The masters then knelt at the head table, then the sensei at their table, and then finally, the students. The masters all looked like they were in their seventies and eighties, Kayla guessed. They certainly didn't look frail however; they all looked exceedingly capable Kayla thought.

Kayla and Ling talked for a long time that night about the masters and about how they would be watched for two weeks. All of the sudden, there was a real deadline, and students would be asked to leave if they didn't impress the masters. Kayla not only worried about her own selection by a master now, but also worried about Ling making the selection too. Both girls had come to realize how much help it was to have a good friend to keep you going during the difficult training. Kayla often couldn't wait to go back to their room in ryokan to complain to Ling about how some sensei had picked on her during the day's training sessions. She found it comforting to find that often Ling also had difficult times, and she was not the only one messing up, or being picked on. It was invaluable to have someone who understood and could relate to what she was going through. Kayla knew she would miss that if Ling didn't make it.

It was unlikely, out of twenty-six students, that both of them would be selected by a master. None of the students got a good sleep that night, all worried about what the masters would make of them and who would be chosen.

The morning run up the mountain was frantic that morning. Everyone wanted to be first and no one wanted to be in the bottom positions. The masters stood waiting at the bottom for them today! It was like starting all over again, having to impress a new set of people. As Kayla crossed the courtyard she heard, 'Nine.' she was pleased with that, she needed to be in the top ten of everything if she wanted to be chosen. Kayla turned to look back for Ling, who she knew was behind her slightly. Ling crossed at position eleven. Kayla so wanted herself and Ling to be chosen!

The masters really pushed the students the first day to see if they could get anyone to quit. Kayla didn't think anyone would quit at this point in the training. The students that were left now were tough. They'd already been through a lot. As soon as the morning run completed, the students were commanded to get the water buckets and yokes from the well. All the students stood in a large circle in the courtyard, with the heavy water yokes across their shoulders, the chief sensei commanded, 'Kiba dachi kamaete'. All the students went into a low horse stance, water slopping out of the buckets that hung to each side of them, as they took up the position. 'If you come up from your kiba dachi you will be asked to leave.' the chief sensei announced. Kayla thought this extremely unfair, but guessed they had to start weeding out students somehow. Kayla knew she could stay in kiba dachi for hours with no problem, however with the heavy water yoke across her shoulders she was quite unsure how long she could last before her legs would give out on her. The students stared out at each other and waited to see who would be the first to quit or collapse. Kayla could feel her legs quivering under the strain they were under after about an hour, however she could see others around her that looked in worse condition than her. The guy next to her was shifting about in his stance and his legs were shaking really badly. About ten minutes later he collapsed, his legs just giving out on him. Water splashed everywhere as his buckets hit the stones. The guy groaned, grabbing his thighs, which probably had cramped up on him. Kayla was praying that the chief would call yame now, but it carried on until another student collapsed. Finally, Kayla thought about ninety minutes or so into the ordeal, the chief called yame and the students remaining slowly came up from kiba dachi and moved around a bit. No one removed the water yokes until they were told to. They were given about five minutes to shake their legs out, take the yokes off, and relieve their shoulders and backs before the chief ordered the yokes back on and then shouted, 'zenkusu dachi, kamaete' and the remaining students took up a deep front stance. The ordeal continued, the students still in a circle watching each other wondering who would be the next to yield. By the end of the day, six more students had left the program, only because their bodies had let them down and collapsed under the strain of deep stances, with a huge amount of weight across their shoulders. Kayla was grateful her body had not let her down. Several times she felt her legs tremor and she didn't know how she stayed standing, but she had.

The competition was fierce. Everyone up'd their game a bit, knowing this was the final push. It seemed to Kayla to be the longest two weeks of her life.

At morning bow in, exactly two weeks later, both students and sensei sat facing the standing masters at the front. The chief sensei told the students what would happen. 'Each master has selected which student they wish to train. If you name is called by a master come to them and kneel in seiza in front of them. Those of you whose names are not called, we congratulate you for making it through a tough training camp. You are all top notch martial artists and none of you sitting before us today needs to feel ashamed about your performance or standard. You can leave with your head held high.' This was it, the moment everyone had been working for almost seven months now. Each master, in turn, called out one student's name. Both Kayla and Ling still sat kneeling when six names had already been called out. Kayla was starting to feel huge disappointment already as she sat waiting. The seventh master, Master Harrington, a woman that looked to be in her early seventies, stepped forward and said, 'Kayla'. Kayla nearly jumped out of her skin, and she had a huge grin on her face, as she walked forward and knelt in seiza in front of Master Harrington. As soon as she knelt down, her mind went to Ling, she hoped she would make it. The eighth master step forward and said, 'Raji'. The next master, Master Tagawa, step forward and said 'Ling'. Kayla grin returned to her face as she watched, with her peripheral vision, Ling going and kneeling in front of Master Tagawa.

There were no celebrations or hoopla. When the final master named his student, the students that were left behind bowed out and went back to their ryokans to pack and leave. The masters each took their students to their own personal dojos to start their training with them. Kayla's master began with a long list of problems she'd seen in Kayla while she watched her train and also imparted some of the senseis' criticisms of her. Kayla's high at being chosen quickly departed as she sat kneeling in front of Master Harrington listening to all her faults. Kayla had always felt uncomfortable sitting in seiza for long periods and had to shift her feet a little at times to keep them from going to sleep. Her master noticed and told Kayla she had a week to train herself to stop fidgeting in seiza. She criticized her for getting this far in the program and still being so sloppy in etiquette. Kayla was upset, she thought her etiquette was impeccable. After sitting for over an hour listening to her all her faults, it was clear to Kayla that the masters were going to be very, very demanding. The program was about to get harder.

Chapter 10

'What did you do?' Kayla queried Ling. As Kayla had bowed out from her afternoon training session with her master and walked through the courtyard back toward the ryokan, she saw Ling out in the courtyard by herself doing Tekki Sandan over and over again. She figured she wouldn't see Ling back in the room for a while. She was right, it was now hours later and Ling had just come in.

Ling crashed down onto the futon on the floor exhausted. She looked up at Kayla and said, 'god, sometimes I'm so stupid.' she paused a moment and then continued, 'Master Tagawa had me doing all the Tekki katas all morning and afternoon in the dojo. I must have done Tekki Sandan about thirty or forty times and every time I finished he would tell me I did something wrong and to do it again. I lost my temper and talked back to him. I told him my hand position was correct and he was seeing things, when he told me I got it wrong once again. Then, if that wasn't bad enough, I complained to him I didn't like doing kata, that kumite was much better to practice.'

Kayla just replied, 'hmmm', knowing herself what trouble she'd been in for doing stuff like that with her master.

Ling continued, 'I got about an hour lecture on why kata is an important part of karate and how I needed to practice kata to get a balance and harmony in my karate that I lacked. He then told me that he couldn't teach me anymore today, my mind was closed. He ordered me to go find my balance and to go out to the courtyard and do each Tekki kata one hundred times on my own. I think I wore a rut in those damn stones out there!'

Kayla smiled and said sarcastically, 'Well, did you find your balance?'

Ling replied, 'Don't mess with me, I'm too tired.' she paused and then said with amusement, 'See if I give you any sympathy the next time you get in trouble!'

Kayla replied, 'If you hurry and change you can still make dinner. Come on.'

The dining arrangements had changed again, the sensei and students now sat at the same long table together, while the masters sat at the head table. The dining hall still had over thirty people in it, but compared to the earlier months with more students and also more sensei, it seemed empty now. As Kayla sat enjoying her dinner and the good conversation she shifted, as she always did, a very small amount to keep her feet from falling asleep. 'Kayla!' she heard her

master's voice from across the dining hall, 'leave the dining hall immediately...
Go change into your gi, and wait for me outside.'

Kayla felt so embarrassed getting up and leaving the dining hall with everyone
watching her, wondering what she had done. Kayla had an idea of what she'd
done, but her shift in seiza was so slight, no one had ever even noticed it before.
Kayla changed quickly into her gi and went back to stand outside the dining
hall, waiting for her master to finish her dinner. Master Harrington emerged
from the dining hall and said calmly to her, 'I told you you had one week to
train yourself to sit in seiza properly. What have you done to train yourself?'

Kayla replied, 'I'm sorry master, I was so tired after the hard day's training
sessions I didn't have time, and I forgot to work on my seiza posture.'

Kayla's master told her to go fetch a shinai from the dojo and bring it back to
her. A shinai is used for kendo practice. It is a flexible bamboo stick that allows
kendo practitioners, dressed in their full armor, to strike each other, imitating a
sword. Being struck by the shinai hurt a bit, but did no permanent damage to
the one being struck. Kayla had heard the long, loud kiai, and the clashing of
the shinai, as the masters and sensei trained in kendo in the late afternoons,
after they had dismissed their students. Kayla held the shinai out with both
hands, offering it to her master with a bow. Her master ordered, 'Seiza'. Kayla
knelt down, just outside the dining hall where all the students, sensei, and
masters were exiting from the evening meal. Everyone knew Kayla was in
trouble since she was sent from the hall early by her master. Now Kayla knelt
outside the hall while her master stood above her, lightly striking her with the
shinai. 'Next time I tell you to do something I suggest you follow my
instructions.' her master said as she walked around Kayla, on her knees, lightly
hitting her with the bamboo stick.

Kayla quickly replied, 'Oss master.' Kayla was not physically hurt by the shinai
strikes, but she felt humiliated, with all her peers and instructors watching her
master disciplining her for not following her instructions. After a time her
master stopped striking Kayla with the shinai and told Kayla to get up. 'Since
you seem incapable of training yourself as I asked, I shall instruct you on how
you will fix your seiza. Until you stop your fidgeting, you will report to the dojo
one hour before we bow in at sunrise. You will sit in seiza and focus your mind
for that hour. Do you understand?'

Kayla quickly replied 'Oss master.'

Kayla was glad she had Ling to talk to. It seemed Ling's master was as
demanding and equally un-easy to please as her master was. The masters were
pushing their students to perfection, picking up on any small flaw in their
karate, or in their character, and attempting to fix it. The girls often discussed

whose master was meaner and tougher on them. They both knew their masters were helping them to become better martial artist and better people, but sometimes the lessons seemed a bit extreme. Kayla had come to the conclusion that her master didn't believe she was capable of remembering anything unless the lesson involved some pain. Maybe she was right, Kayla reflected, thinking it would be a long time before she ignored her master's instructions again after tonight! Ling had to admit, after watching Kayla be humiliated after dinner tonight for the minor transgression of a shift in her seiza position, that possibly Kayla's master was meaner than hers. Before she admitted this however, she took the opportunity to tease her friend, 'Well, it didn't take you long to get into more trouble than me. Thanks, you made me feel a lot better.' Ling giggled. Kayla did explain to Ling that Master Harrington was probably more upset with her because she had ignored her instructions to train herself than the minor breach of etiquette. Kayla felt she probably deserved what she got actually. Although Kayla often thought Master Harrington's methods were extreme, she had to admit, they worked. Kayla knew she was improving quickly under Master Harrington's tutelage.

Chapter 11

Once a week, the remaining students were required to teach a class. Their 'students' were the sensei, and their masters sat watching the class. Ling and Kayla both found this task a bit daunting. Not only were they being scrutinized by their masters, but teaching a group of highly experienced sensei was difficult and nerve racking for the students. Ling especially found it difficult, being so young and never having run a class on her own before. Kayla had a bit more experience running a class, as she often taught classes for her sensei at her home dojo. But Kayla also found the pressure of teaching her sensei unnerving, especially with Master Harrington sitting there watching her every move. The students were told to teach the sensei as they would any other student and not as their teachers during the class.

'Ling, did you not see Sensei Komhara leave the dojo to get water?' Master Tagawa queried Ling, who was teaching her weekly class.

'Oss master.' Ling replied.

'He did not ask your permission, and also did not bow out. Why did you let him get away with that?'

Ling knew Sensei Komhara had done this on purpose. The irony was not lost on her. Months earlier she was rightly accused of disrespecting him; now she was the teacher, and he was testing her, to see what she would do when one of her students didn't show the proper respect or follow the rules of the dojo. Ling replied, 'Sorry master, I find it difficult to admonish my sensei, it is not my place.'

Master Tagawa replied, 'Normally you are correct Ling, but did we not tell you you must treat your sensei as normal students during this class. This class is to help you learn to become a good teacher yourself. You must learn to criticize and correct your students or your students will never change or get better.'

Ling really didn't like being the teacher and the one in charge. She was perfectly happy to be the one being criticized, well, most of the time, but she was uncomfortable being the one doing the criticizing. Especially to Sensei Komhara, who still scared her a bit. Ling could see her master was waiting for her to do something about the situation. 'Sensei Komhara, you must ask for permission before you leave the class. If you are given permission, you must bow out of the dojo before you leave it.' Ling looked very uncomfortable as she spoke to Sensei Komhara.

Sensei Komhara replied, 'Oss', bowed to Ling, and returned to the line.

Ling breathed a huge sigh of relief when the class finally finished. One other sensei had tested her again during the class, by talking back to her when she corrected his obvious, intentional mistake. This time she recognized the test and told him politely to adjust his attitude and listen to her correction. Ling smiled to herself, thinking, 'and if I was Master Tagawa, you'd be out doing that kata in the courtyard hundreds of times by yourself for the rest of the afternoon.'

When Ling got back to the room later that afternoon Kayla queried her roommate, 'How did teaching go today?'

Ling replied, 'Well, Sensei Komhara didn't show me any respect today, so I got right up in his face and said, "You show me no respect Sensei Komhara" and told him to go climb the dojo stairs with the water buckets.' Ling said this with a completely straight face.

Kayla was taken in for a moment and started to say, 'What!' but then realized Ling was pulling her leg and laughed along with her.

Chapter 12

Kayla felt her ribs crack as she missed the block and the sensei's side thrust kick slammed into her side. 'Ahhh...', Kayla moaned as she fell to the dojo floor holding her side.

The sensei she was sparring with said, 'Stand up Kayla.' Kayla was in great pain but stood, still holding her stomach and ribs. 'Take off your jacket and let me see.', the sensei said. Kayla slipped off her gi jacket and the sensei felt her ribs. 'They are bruised, not broken.' he said rather nonchalantly and uncaringly, Kayla thought. 'Go fetch the tape and I'll bind them up.'

Kayla stood with her hands on her head as the sensei wrapped tape around her ribs. As soon as he completed taping he said, 'Put your jacket back on and we will continue.' Kayla was shocked he wanted to continue sparring while she was clearly injured. She was even more shocked when he didn't ease off and hit her with a reverse punch in the ribs. Kayla dropped down to her knees, 'Ahhh.' She looked up at him with a look like ,'what the hell are you doing?' Kayla's master, who sat watching all this said, 'Kayla, when you are injured you must not show your weaknesses to your opponent. It is your responsibility, not your opponent's, to protect your injuries.'

Kayla got up saying 'Oss master.' and took up her fighting position again. Now she realized this was yet another test, about how one handles one's self when injured. It was probably no accident the sensei had hit her just hard enough to badly bruise her ribs, but do no serious damage. She knew now the sensei would not worry about her ribs, but she must be sure to protect them herself. As she was fighting, Kayla kept her injured side away from the sensei and was cautious not to expose her side on any attacks. She started only defending herself and stopped attacking.

'Yame.', Master Harrington called and both fighters stopped and faced the master. 'Kayla, although you are now protecting your injuries, you are showing weakness by not attacking.'

Kayla's anger was rising inside her, 'god, what did this woman want from her?' Kayla kept her anger under control and replied, 'Master, I don't understand what you want me to do?'

Master Harrington explained, 'Protect your injuries, as you have been doing, but you must still look for openings to attack. Sensei Taylor gave you several opportunities to attack him and you did not, because you were afraid to hurt yourself again. Do you understand?'

Kayla replied, 'Oss master.', bowed and took up her fighting position again with the sensei.

When Kayla got back to her room after training that day, her ribs aching, she slid back the screen to see Ling sitting on the floor with packing up her swollen nose, a fat, split lip, and blood stains down the front of her gi. Kayla looked at her friend and said, 'The lesson of how to fight when you are injured?'

Ling replied sarcastically, 'How did you guess?'

Kayla undid the flap of her jacket and showed Ling her taped ribs and said, 'bruised ribs for me.'

Ling told Kayla how the sensei she was sparring with had cracked her on the nose. 'Seeing my own blood on my gi really pissed me off.' Ling told Kayla. 'I flew in at him with anger and before I knew it, he popped me in the nose again! ... on purpose!' Ling smirked, but then grimaced in pain with her split lip. 'I didn't learn the lesson the first time, so I grew more outraged and again fought harder and with more fury. Before I knew it, I had a fat lip to match my bloody nose.' Ling paused, then signed and said, 'Ya know Kayla, sometimes I'm such a slow learner, I think Master Tagawa felt sorry for me... before I could fly into another outrageous attack he stopped us and told me to stop fighting with fury and anger and use my head. He probably saved me getting a broken nose from Sensei Moreita for my stupid outrageous attacks I was throwing at him... I realized then, only because I was told, that I exposed all my weaknesses when I fight with anger rather than a calm, clear mind.' Kayla thought to herself how differently she'd reacted to getting hurt. She'd gone into a defensive, self-protection mode and shut down. She'd been encouraged to get out there and attack again, while Ling reacted with rage and needed to be taught to calm herself down and fight a smart fight. Kayla was very impressed with the masters that were teaching them, they really knew how to expose their student's weaknesses and help them to overcome them.

Chapter 13

Kayla sat watching the mountain stream, recalling all her many experiences she had had since she arrived here. As she thought back over the months of training, she realized now how much she had learnt about herself in these few short months. When she arrived at camp, she really didn't think she could learn much more than she already knew, after years of training in the martial arts, but these teachers were really good. Not only had she improved her physical skills with the constant training, but mostly she was a stronger person now. She had learned to control her temper, to be humble, to take pain and not show it, to endure when you think you can go on no more, and now, the final lesson, to have an indomitable spirit at all times. Her master exemplified all these things. 'God that woman was so impressive' Kayla thought as she reflected on the sparring match she'd just lost to the seventy year old woman. As Kayla rose from the rock, she knew she had the spirit to finish what she had started. It had been a painful process, but so far, she'd managed to learn the many lessons her master and sensei had taught her. This lesson had taken more than one or two tries to learn, but her master had been patient with her... up until today! Kayla felt strong and confident now. She was going to make her master proud of her.

Kayla now believed in herself and her skills when she entered the dojo the next morning. Master Harrington's words rang in her ears as she waited for her to arrive, 'If you set foot back in this dojo unprepared again, you will be sorry.' Kayla sat quietly in seiza, mentally preparing herself for facing her master, and whatever challenges she was going to face today. Master Harrington entered and they bowed in together.

'Kayla, I am pleased to see you are not a quitter. I have pushed you very hard the last few months. Many people quit on me before the first month is over, but you have found the inner strength to carry on and continue your training.' Kayla was amazed; this was the first compliment she'd ever received from her master. 'Are you ready to face your test today?' she asked. Kayla did not hesitate, and felt an inner strength that was not false this morning, and said quickly, 'Oss master.'

'Yame.' Master Harrington called as Kayla floored the sensei she was sparring with and was going in for the final blow to finish him off. Kayla stopped, with her fist drawn back ready to punch, and uncurled her first to offer her hand to the sensei on the floor. Kayla's master looked her in the eye and said, 'Well done Kayla.' Kayla had never heard those words from her master's lips before and she broke out in a huge smile. Kayla had taken on many opponents today, she hadn't won every round, and she found herself on the dojo floor just as many times as the other day, but this time her inner spirit had never waivered. With each new opponent Kayla was able to clear her mind and find her remaining spirit, her zanshin, to begin each new challenge with strength and clarity of purpose.

'Thank you master.' Kayla said still smiling.

'Don't let it go to your head.' Master Harrington said, half joking but half serious as well. Kayla was still smiling as she cleaned the dojo floor after bow out. Cleaning her master's dojo was part of her responsibilities now that there were only ten students remaining in the program.

Chapter 14

As the autumn arrived, Kayla realized it would soon be time for the selection of the final five students who would become WKIA sensei. None of the students knew how the selection would happen or when exactly. No one had the guts to ask their masters any questions regarding selection process. Since the final ten students were selected, no one had dropped out and no one had been kicked out either, so there was still only a fifty-fifty chance of attaining her goal Kayla realized. When the program first began, and during winter training, Kayla couldn't wait for the training to be over, but now that the finish line was in sight, she never wanted it to end. She didn't want to lose her adopted little sister Ling, or her master, who was like a very tough, stern mother and father all rolled into one. They had been her family for the past year now. The whole group that was left was a fantastic group of highly dedicated people, and Kayla didn't want things to change. And change they would, the five new sensei would go out to wherever the WKIA assigned them to. Each new sensei would be expected to run one of the WKIA dojos somewhere, anywhere, in the world that they were assigned. They would need to live and work to further the martial arts and the WKIA in that area of the world. If Kayla and Ling both became sensei, they would not have much time to see each other, being based in different areas of the world.

Since the masters had taken their own students, the students had not fought against each other, but with the sensei. A tournament was arranged for the remaining students. Everyone assumed the top five students from the tournament would be awarded the sensei title. The night before the tournament Ling and Kayla sat up talking. They each could have had their own room now at the ryokan, with only ten students left, but they chose to stay together still. They both liked having someone to chat to. They discussed all the possibilities of what might happen at the tournament, who they might have to fight, and on and on. Neither of them slept good that night worrying about the next day.

The masters sat in chairs surrounding the parameter of the largest dojo. The students sat kneeling along the edge also. The chief sensei was the centre referee and called two students up at a time for kumite. No points were called and the fighting was not stopped until one of the masters would call yame. It was difficult to determine who was winning or losing at times, and no one seemed to be keeping track of the rounds or points, although Kayla knew the masters all had very sharp minds and probably kept track in their heads. Kayla and Ling both had a few rounds each before they were called to fight each other. The girls bowed to each other and took up their fighting positions. Ling, who had been trained mostly in kung-fu was difficult to fight against because of her unorthodox circular striking patterns and she loved close up, hand-to-hand techniques. Where Kayla, coming mostly from Japanese styles, wanted distance from her opponent and to throw strong straight punches and kicks. It made for an interesting match. For minutes the match was equal, but then Ling stepped in close and got Kayla into a fast moving set of hand techniques. Kayla missed a block and found herself floored by an upper cut that took her breath away and knocked her down to her knees. Before Kayla could catch her breath and get out of the way, Ling finished her off with a side snap kick under the chin knocking her to the floor. Kayla was quickly getting up to continue when 'Yame.' was called. The girls bowed to each other and went back to kneel. Kayla couldn't believe Ling beat her! She was disappointed she'd lost, but after watching Ling fight all day today she realized now Ling was probably the best fighter at the camp! The tournament finished and nothing was said about the outcome or who won or anything, they just bowed out as normal.

While getting ready for dinner that night Kayla complimented Ling on her fighting skills. 'You are amazing Ling, I think you won the tournament today.'

Ling smiled at her friend and said, 'How's your jaw?'

Kayla had a black and blue mark under her chin from the side snap kick her friend had administered during their bout. 'Well, I'm glad you have good control and I had a gum shield in or I'd be eating my dinner through a straw tonight.' Kayla smiled and then winced as smiling hurt her jaw.

That evening at dinner, just after they bowed to the masters standing at the front of the hall, one of the masters said, 'Tomorrow, for the first time since you have arrived here, we are giving you a day off. We,' referring to the masters around him, 'will take this evening and all day tomorrow to discuss with the sensei and each other, who is to be appointed the title of sensei. Students may do what they please tomorrow. The following morning at bow in we will announce our decision.'

All the students glanced around at each other, all wondering who would be the lucky ones to get appointed Sensei. Kayla really wished she had performed better at the tournament, but she never let her spirit stop her, she was just up against the best martial artists in the world. Kayla hoped her kata, which she'd worked very hard to perfect, might serve to boost her above her fellow students, many of whom she spotted small flaws in their kata performances.

The free day was torture. There was not much to do at the camp except train really. The students found the day long, wondering what their sensei and masters were saying about them. All Kayla could think about was the long list of problems her master had communicated to her the first day she was chosen. She wondered now how successful she had been at correcting all her faults over the last few months. She certainly could not have given any more than she had. This program had pushed Kayla right to her limits, and on reflection Kayla thought there was nothing more she could have given. Her master had pushed her beyond where Kayla herself thought she was capable of going. Kayla thought she eventually had been molded into the martial artist her master wanted her to be, but she wondered now if it had taken her too long to get there and if she'd racked up too many black marks along the way. Kayla's mind started tormenting her in the middle of the sleepless night, reminding her of all her failures along the long way. Kayla was sure she did not sleep a wink that night, and neither did Ling, or any of the other students left.

Everyone was up and dressed in their gis early for bow in the next morning. As they waited in attention for the masters to emerge, the tension was high.

The students and sensei sat in seiza while the masters stood at the front, 'I want to begin by congratulating every one of you for completing this program. It is a great achievement of which you can be immensely proud. Even if you are not granted the title of WKIA sensei today, you can go away knowing you are amongst the best of the best, and the sensei and masters here will always help you in your endeavors. We always regret that we cannot grant everyone the title of sensei, however keeping the numbers low ensures quality and keeps the special nature of the WKIA sensei.' He paused and looked around. 'I will call, one at a time, each person who has achieved the sensei appointment. If your name is called, rise, and come sit in seiza in the front here.'

Kayla was nervous sitting waiting...three names had already been called out. The fourth called was 'Devindra.' Kayla was disappointed, there was only one slot left and both she and Ling had not been called. She knew Ling would get the slot over her because Ling was the best fighter in the group. The final name was called out, 'Kayla.' Kayla was shocked. She was very happy, but couldn't believe she got the slot over Ling.

Master Harrington stood above Kayla and said, 'Kiritsu Sensei Kayla.' Kayla rose to attention. 'Please remove your white belt.' her master said as she stood holding out the WKIA Sensei's black belt to her student. Kayla bowed deeply as she took the belt from her master and put it around her waist. After all the new sensei had their black belts on they turned to face the remaining students and the chief sensei commanded, 'Sensei ni rei.' and the five remaining students bowed to the new sensei. Kayla was both ecstatically happy and also very sad watching Ling bow to her. The students were dismissed and the new sensei went off with their masters to their dojos.

Kayla knelt before her master again as she spoke. 'Kayla, I'm very proud of you. You will make a very fine sensei.'

Kayla replied, 'Thank you master.' she hesitated and then said, 'Master, may I ask a question of you?' Her master nodded her head. 'Ling is a much better fighter than I. She beat me, and many of the other students, the other day at the kumite. Why was she not selected above me?'

Her master replied, 'Kayla, you know being a good sensei is much more than being a good fighter. Ling is young and somewhat impetuous in nature. She did very well to stay in the program to the end. Many of the sensei thought her temper would get the better of her and that she was incapable of changing. We actually put you two together in the ryokan on purpose, knowing Ling would need help and a good influence on her. Sensei Komhara was surprised when you two fought the first night, but he had overhead you trying to avoid the fight several times and was impressed how you handled her. Your ability to influence the people around you is one of the many skills we look for in our sensei.'

Kayla couldn't believe it, she thought she'd made a horrible first impression with Sensei Komhara, but he had known she'd tried her best to avoid the fight.

Master Harrington continued, 'I pushed you very hard Kayla, to test your character. We not only look for talented martial artists to be our sensei, but we need our sensei to be of outstanding character. "Strive for perfection of character", after all is our first imperative of our training. You probably don't realize it yet, but the evening I sent you from the dining hall and struck you with my shinai was one of my most difficult tests of a student's character.'
Kayla had not realized it was a test at all, but now smiled to herself thinking she was not the first student to be struck by Master Harrington's shinai.

Kayla's master continued, 'For this test I look for something my student is proud of in his or her self. For you, I could see you have impeccable etiquette and are very proud of that. So I chose this to test your character. I wanted to see how you would handle a relatively unfair criticism of something you were highly proud of and then push you to see how you would react to the quite unfair dressing down I subjected you to outside the dining hall.'

Kayla thought to herself, 'so that's what she calls a "dressing down". She had to give Master Harrington credit; she was a very fine actress. Kayla never guessed her master was remotely pleased with her what-so-ever up until just a few days ago, when she finally got her first complement after months of training with her. She had pushed Kayla to her limits right up till the last day of training! "Bull-dozer Harrington" Kayla thought and smiled to herself.

Her master continued, 'Many students fail at this test, their anger flares and they lose spirit and confidence in themselves. You passed my test with flying colors. You showed humility when accepting my dressing down and you tried even harder to fix the minor flaw I had pointed out to you. You never once asked me to lift my command that you come to the dojo an hour before sunrise to sit in seiza; even when you'd stopped your fidgeting. You did not get angry or lose confidence in your self; you just tried very hard to fix what was wrong. Humility, patience, perseverance, and dedication are what every martial artist should possess, but these qualities are absolute necessities for a successful sensei, Kayla. A sensei must be humble or she will stop learning. Once you think you know it all, it is time to quit, so humility is a key quality to continue to learn. Patience and perseverance are required of a sensei too. You will have students who will test this every time they enter your dojo. You must have endless patience to teach a technique or kata to a student over and over and over when they just can't remember it or get it right. Many students will not be as committed or dedicated to the art as you would like them to be and this will also try you. Finally, dedication is required to keep train yourself, to keep motivated, and to keep your dojo going day in and day out. You have demonstrated to me and the other instructors you have all these qualities Kayla. That is why you were chosen over some of the other students. You friend Ling is a very fine martial artist but she is young and still has some lessons to learn. She still needs to be taught rather than being the teacher. In time she will make a fine teacher I am sure, but she is not ready yet. Your friend Ling will be fine Kayla, you need not worry about her'. She paused and said, 'Now, back to you Sensei Kayla. Your first assignment as a new WKIA sensei is going to be Beijing. We have not had a sensei in China before so you will be responsible for introducing WKIA karate to this part of the world.'

Kayla was excited about this, but was still thinking of Ling. 'Master, may I take an assistant with me to help me?'

Her master saw where she was going with this, 'Yes, if you wish to take Ling with you to help you; that would be good.' Kayla and her master talked for a long time. When Kayla walked out of the dojo hours later, she looked down at the WKIA black belt around her waist and smiled... she'd done it!

Chapter 15

As Kayla slid back the screen to her room she saw Ling sitting on the floor, just starring out into space. Ling moved into seiza, bowed, and sincerely said 'Oss Sensei.' with a grin on her face, happy for her friend.

Kayla bowed back and said, 'Thanks Ling.' Kayla continued, 'What are your plans now?'

Ling looked dejected, 'I have no idea Kayla. I'd love to stay here actually.'

Kayla smiled and said, 'How would you like to be my assistant?'

Ling looked up hopefully, 'Really?'

Kayla said, 'Yes, I will need lots of help and I cannot think of a better person to help me that you my friend.' she smiled.

Ling had a big grin on her face as she said, 'Kayla, you have no idea... you just saved my life.'

Kayla thought she was being a bit over dramatic but then said, 'Good, we can stay here a few more nights, and then we are off to Beijing.'

Ling's face dropped, 'What... Beijing?' she queried Kayla.

'Yes, I've been given Beijing as my first assignment.' Kayla said excitedly.

Ling dropped her head down into her hands, 'I can't do it., she was crying.

Kayla was shocked, she'd never seen Ling cry over anything. Kayla dropped down to her friend crying into her hands and put her hand on her shoulder and said, 'What is it Ling? Why can't you do it?'

Ling looked up at Kayla, tears streaming down her face, 'I don't want to tell you, you'll be disappointed with me.'

Kayla replied, 'Come on Ling, it can't be that bad. You can tell me anything.' Kayla realized as she said this that although Ling and she had become the best of friends, Ling had never told her what had happened to her family, or any more about her background or life. They had spent hours discussing their training and fellow students, but Ling had never opened up to Kayla and told her about herself. Kayla realized she still knew very little about Ling.

Ling began in a quiet voice, 'I grew up in Beijing. My parents gave me up when I was a baby because I was the first born child, and a girl. This is what I was told anyway; I never knew them.' Ling was struggling with her words. Kayla could see she was clearly terrified to tell her whatever it was she was about to say. 'I grew up in an orphanage. They are probably unlike orphanages in America Kayla; they are horrible, overcrowded places where you had to fight for food and even a bed sometimes. I hated every moment of it. The only thing that kept me going in the orphanage was a kung-fu master that came to train the children there, Sifu Suxi. I was his favorite student because I was talented at kung-fu and I always turned up everyday for training, no matter what.' Ling paused, clearly thinking carefully of what she wanted to tell Kayla now, 'When I was fifteen years old I ran away from the orphanage. I just couldn't stand it there anymore and wanted to take my chances in the real world. It didn't take long before I found out the real world was really a tough, horrible place if you're a kid with no money or anywhere to live. I had no where to go and I was completely and utterly lost. As most kids on the streets of Beijing do, I found a gang to join. The gang gave me an instant family, a place to hang out, and a way to survive.' Ling briefly looked up from the floor she'd been staring at to look at Kayla and then continued, 'Unfortunately, the gang also gave me a nasty drug habit and, ultimately, got me in trouble with the police.' Kayla thought back to her initial assessment of Ling on the first day they met and knew she had been right about Ling, tough life, street- wise girl that reminded her of the gang bangers she'd worked with before.

As Ling paused Kayla piped up and said,
'Ling, this is not that bad. You were young, you did what you had to do. You've changed now, that's the important thing.'

Ling looked up and said with sadness in her voice, 'Sensei I am not finished with my story yet.' and continued with trepidation in her voice, 'Do you know how you get jumped into a gang?'

Kayla replied, 'I believe that involves the establish gang members giving the new initiate a good beating. The new member has to stand her ground and show no fear - correct?'

Ling was quite surprised Kayla knew anything about gangs and replied, 'Ya, that's pretty much it. Well, when I was jumped in, I managed to not only hold my ground, but I also took out a few of the established gang members during the fight. Although the leader of the gang was impressed with my skills, my ability to avoid the beating they wanted to give me caused them to issue me a new initiation task; they called it "blood in". I had to kill a member of our rival gang now to prove myself.'

Kayla tensed, but sat still, waiting to see what Ling would say next, but Ling just sat starring at the floor, not wanting to continue.

Kayla decided to save her friend from the pain of carrying on, 'Ling, everything you are telling me is in the past. You are not that person anymore. Do you believe you have changed?' Kayla looked at her friend.

Ling looked up to face Kayla and said, 'Yes, I am a completely different person to who I was then and even to the person I was a year ago when I started this program.' she gulped and continued, 'but some things cannot be forgiven or undone Kayla.'

Kayla replied, 'I agree that things can never be undone, but forgiven is not impossible.' she paused then and asked, 'How did you get into this program?'

Ling answered Kayla question, but avoided telling Kayla how she had finally proven herself to get into the gang, 'I was finally initiated into the gang. It was our standard practice to fund ourselves by robbing people on the streets. One night, I was really out of it on drugs, and didn't even notice a group of police officers right down the street from where I decided to beat up a guy for his wallet. The police came after me and really beat the hell out of me with their truncheons when they arrested me. I can't remember much of what happened that night, but the next day when I awoke in a jail cell, I had a broken nose, ribs, and arm. I was charged with assault, robbery, carrying a weapon, and resisting arrest. They really threw the book at me because they knew I was a gang member. I sat in jail for weeks awaiting trial. One day my sifu from the orphanage came and visited me. I was a wreck Kayla; I had been shooting up on heroin for months and had to detox cold turkey in jail. I cannot tell you how painful it is to be throwing your guts up when you have broken ribs. Being stuck in that overcrowded jail cell, beaten up and coming off heroin was pure hell on earth. By the time sifu came to see me I was at rock bottom; all my street bravado and unclear, drug-induced thinking was gone by then. I begged for his help, which, had he come a few weeks earlier I probably wouldn't have had the sense to do. He told me he would help me and that gave me the strength to carry on. It turns out my sifu is a pretty influential man in Beijing and when I went to trial he managed to convince the judge that he would take responsibility for me, take me away from Beijing and the gang, and sort me out. I had already been in jail for a few weeks awaiting trial so the judge let me go with sifu, but told me never to set foot in Beijing again. Sifu took me out to the country and started training me again, this time in karate rather than kung-fu. After the slow and painful detox from heroin in jail, and the very real possibility I faced of being sent to a labor camp, or worse; I did everything I could to sort myself out, stay off the drugs, and train hard. Sifu somehow got me signed up for this program and put me here to continue the rehabilitation he had started me on.

Kayla looked seriously at her friend, 'Ling, if I took you back to Beijing would you be tempted to go back to the gang or back to drugs?'

Ling immediately shot back 'No sensei, no way, I will never ever go back to that life.'

Kayla smiled at her friend, 'Well then, I need to speak with your sifu to discuss how we can get you back to Beijing. Ling, your experiences would be useful if we started a gang outreach program. Perhaps we can work with your sifu to help other kids, like you used to be.'

Ling looked at her friend and said, 'I can see why they made you a sensei.'

Chapter 16
Beijing, China

Kayla, Sifu Suxi, and Ling stood before a Beijing court judge in his small, unimpressive office. He clearly was not an important judge, but probably dealt with petty cases. Although petty cases in China were sometimes dealt with pretty severely, Kayla thought. This judge had the power to banish Ling from her home town for a mere assault and robbery charge, so she did not underestimate the power of the small man that sat before them. Sifu Suxi spoke at great length with the judge, but Kayla was at a loss, as she did not speak much Chinese yet. Eventually Ling turned to Kayla and said, 'The judge wishes to know if you will be responsible for me and my actions.'

Kayla responded and Ling translated for her, 'The young woman who stands before you today is not the same young girl who stood trial before you a year and a half ago. I have watched her grow and mature and I am fully confident she will make a great contribution to society. Yes, I unreservedly agree to take responsibility for her and her actions.'

The judge started talking to Ling now and, although Kayla couldn't understand what he said, she could tell from the tone of his voice and his demeanor that he was giving her a stern warning. Ling stood with her hands clasped in front of her, Kayla thought trying her best to look repentant, nodding and agreeing with the judge speaking to her. A few moments later the three were walking out of the judge's office and Kayla asked Ling, 'What did he say?'

Ling replied, 'Difficult to translate it all, but basically I'm on probation and you and sifu are responsible for me.'

Kayla smiled, 'So you can come home to Beijing then?'

Ling smiled back and threw her arms around both her sifu and Kayla and said, 'Yes, I can come home thanks to you two.' then she said it again in Chinese for her sifu.

Chapter 17

Kayla and Ling got to work finding a cheap location to setup a dojo. Kayla had not been given a very large budget by the WKIA to start a completely new dojo. She had also completely underestimated how difficult this task would be. Beijing was a huge city, she couldn't speak the language, and the Chinese method of hunting for and securing a property was completely foreign to her. Ling's knowledge of Beijing and ability to speak fluent Chinese was a huge help to Kayla. In fact, she realized there would be little chance of success without her.

Beijing was no longer the quant bicycle-riding city of old, it was now a polluted, traffic jammed, noisy, large, modern city. Quite often Kayla longed for the peacefulness of the mountains again after a day running around the streets of Beijing! It was so quiet up at the training camp with no electronics, phones, or traffic; only the sound of the birds and the occasional kiai broke the peaceful silence. In the mountains there was nothing to think about but perfecting one's character and the art of karate. One was not bothered with figuring out bus schedules, contracts, and budgets that now distracted Kayla. It was strange going back to normal life again after a year in the mountains. It even felt strange wearing street clothes again after a year in nothing but karate gis and kimonos. The two things Kayla was glad to have back however, were a hot shower and a bed! She thought to herself, 'I will never take being warm and in a comfortable bed for granted again!'

Kayla had been given three months to do what she could to establish the WKIA in Beijing before Master Harrington was to visit and see how things were going. Kayla still wanted to impress her master and was working very hard to try to get things up and running in only three months. Kayla and Ling spent weeks tromping around some of the worst back streets in Beijing looking for a suitable dojo location. It was not easy trying to find some place that was suitable in the budget they had. Eventually Kayla signed a year lease on a place that had potential, but needed a lot of work before it would be ready for students. It was up a narrow back street that was too small for cars to zoom up and down. Beijing was still full of small alleyways like this. Kayla liked being away from the traffic and this area had lots of local residents and small businesses all around. The girls moved out of their hotel and bought some futons in order to move into the small one bedroom hovel that came with the floor space they had rented. The place was depressing. The one room that was living room and bedroom had no windows and was basically a small box that needed a good clean and a paint job. The "kitchen" was a shelf that ran along one side of the living room/bedroom that consisted of a hot plate and a sink which dripped and looked like it hadn't been cleaned in years. There were no cupboards or places to put anything and it appeared the previous residents, who had left all their junk behind, just stacked stuff underneath the shelf. The bathroom was downstairs, attached to the floor space Kayla hoped would one day resemble a dojo, once they cleared all the junk out of it. Kayla looked around and thought, 'So much for my hot shower and bed, that didn't last very long!' but she was excited; this was her dojo now and she knew with a little hard work they could make it a decent place to live and train. The local residents were all intrigued that an American woman had moved into their neighborhood, a first for this poor area of Beijing. There were many Americans around in Beijing these days, but not in these back streets! The girls had lots of visitors welcoming them, curious of what they were doing in this poor area.

Ling and Kayla went to the local market in the alleyways they lived in now to get paint and cleaning supplies to start work on their new place. It was amazing, but everything they needed could be found in this labyrinth of little hovels and market stalls. Kayla loved walking through these little alleyways. The sights, smells, and noises that came from the alleyways and shops were exotic and so foreign to anything she had ever known. Everything posed a challenge in China. Even purchasing cleaning and painting supplies was tricky when she couldn't read the labels or recognize the containers things came in. Once again, Kayla was grateful Ling was with her and could read what was in the containers, because everything was packaged differently than it would have been in the west. Kayla would have never found a can of paint in these back alley shops if Ling had not been able to ask the locals which street vendor might sell paint. There did not appear to be anything like a Home Depot in Beijing yet, and it took the girls several days to track down everything they needed to change the dingy, grimy box they lived in into a home.

Not only could the girls find all the cleaning and do-it-yourself supplies they needed locally, but they also found they could eat and buy groceries in these alleyways too. Although, Kayla wondered if she'd ever learn to enjoy the food here. Ling had bought some noodles and, to Kayla's horror, some live eels from a local merchant. The eels had been fished out of a tank, killed with a large cleaver, and skinned right before them. Ling had whipped up some type of disgusting stir fry with the eels that Kayla could barely choke down. Although Kayla had never been a huge fan of fast food, as she choked down Ling's bad smelling stir fry, she tried to remember where in the touristy part of Beijing they had seen the golden arches! The food pretty much grossed Kayla out and she figured at this rate she'd probably never gain back the ten pounds she'd lost in the mountains. As they wandered through the food markets Kayla found the smells and the look of most of the food unappetizing, to say the least.

The girls spent several days cleaning out the dojo floor space, cleaning walls, and putting fresh paint everywhere. Kayla had a pleasant surprise when she pulled back a grimy, old linoleum tile off the main floor space and found a sold wood floor under the dirty tiles. It was hard work, but she and Ling pulled off all the old linoleum tiles and sanded away, by hand, all the excess junk remaining on the floor. They then sealed the floor with a lovely dark stain. After two weeks of hard work Kayla and Ling stood back and looked at their new dojo and were proud of it.

Master Harrington was due in two weeks time to check on their progress and Kayla was feeling proud of her achievements thus far. But she still had no students! She needed to start advertising now that the dojo was ready. Kayla had Ling make up some leaflets for her. She told her what she wanted on them and Ling translated it into Chinese for her. The girls put the leaflets around the alleyways they lived within. There were hundreds and hundreds of people, all potential students, in this small area.

Kayla and Ling waited in anticipation as they opened the doors to the dojo for the first class. They invited anyone to come in, for the first two weeks of open, free classes hoping to get lots of students in with offer of free lessons. No one turned up. Kayla was so disappointed. Ling explained to Kayla something Kayla already knew about, but had hoped it would not be an issue. The Chinese people had a long and difficult history with the Japanese and tended to dislike any Japanese influence in their land. They loved their kung-fu and Chinese martial arts. Karate was foreign and an unknown to them, as was Kayla, the young American woman teaching it. Unlike the rest of the world, the WKIA meant nothing to Chinese people. They valued older teachers, assuming with age came wisdom and skill, and probably would not accept Kayla had the skills she did being such a young person. Kayla and Ling discussed how they could overcome these issues. Kayla's master was arriving the next day and Kayla so wanted to show her a dojo full of students. She was disappointed, but there was little she could do about it today. Ling saw her friend's disappointment and said, 'Kayla, you've managed to do a lot in three months. You got my problem sorted out so I could come back to Beijing. You found a suitable place for a dojo and look how wonderful we have made it.'

Kayla looked around, 'Ya, we did do a nice job fixing this place up. It looks pretty good now. If only we had students to teach we'd be in business.'

Ling replied, 'Don't worry, we can work on that.'

Chapter 18

That night Kayla awoke with a start. She sat up and listened. She wasn't sure if she was dreaming or if she really had heard something. A second later a crash from downstairs told her she wasn't dreaming. She looked over to Ling's futon to see if it was her crashing around downstairs but it was not; she was sound asleep on her futon still. Kayla got up and nudged Ling with her foot to wake her. Ling groaned and rolled over. Kayla whispered, 'Ling, get up, I think there's someone downstairs in the dojo.' Ling ignored this until another large crash came from downstairs and then she sat bolt upright and looked up at Kayla, who was slipping on her warm-ups to go down and take a look.

Ling said, 'Hey, wait for me.' and got up and slipped her jeans on and followed Kayla down the narrow dark staircase to the dojo below. As Kayla arrived at the bottom of the stairs she saw six figures in hooded jackets smashing up the dojo and throwing paint and, what looked like some time of tar, over the floors. She yelled, 'Get the hell out of here.' and Ling yelled in Chinese at them. All of the figures stopped what they were doing and headed toward the girls. The girls had been trained at taking on multiple attackers and stood back to back in fighting position ready to take on the attackers rushing toward them. Three attackers headed for Kayla and three surrounded Ling. Kayla took the first person to reach her out with a side thrust kick right into his knee cap. This took him out of action screaming in pain on the floor. She was about to launch her next attack on the other two quickly approaching her when she heard Ling scream behind her. Ling's attackers had pulled knives on her and one was across her throat when Kayla glanced over her shoulder at her friend. Kayla saw Ling was bleeding badly from a large slash down her forearm. The teenage boy holding the knife at Ling's throat said something in Chinese to Kayla. Kayla had no idea what he said but realized if she didn't stop her attacks he'd probably slash Ling's throat, so she stopped and put her hands up showing she was not going to continue the fight. Before she knew it, Kayla had a knife across her throat also. Both Kayla and Ling had experience in disarming knife attacks, but both also knew that unless they really thought their attackers were going to kill them, it was not worth the risk, especially with the razor sharp blades at their throats. Kayla thought that these guys only wanted to wreck the dojo and scare them and were not intending on killing them. She looked at her friend and with that glance Ling and Kayla agreed it was not worth the risk and did not resist. Their attackers tied their hands tightly behind their backs. Kayla was forced onto her stomach on the dojo floor while Ling was dragged up the stairs. Kayla started to wonder if she'd made the right decision to stop fighting as she watched Ling being dragged upstairs. The boys left with Kayla tied her feet up and she was left to lie there helplessly watching them continue to destroy her dojo. Kayla pulled her head off the floor and asked, 'Why are you doing this?' Her question was ignored. Kayla could hear the upstairs being

smashed up too and worried about her friend up there. What were they doing to her? A few moments later, Ling came down the stairs first with one the gang behind her with his knife still across her throat. As she reached the bottom stair he released the knife from across the throat and tripped her, pushing her forward. She sprawled face first into the dojo floor unable to catch herself with her hands tied behind her. She groaned when she hit the floor hard. Ling's legs were also tied as she lay next to Kayla on the dojo floor. The guy who Kayla had taken out with a thrust kick to the knee was groaning on the ground still. He seemed to be the one giving the orders; he said something in Chinese to the rest of the gang. Rags were then stuffed into Kayla and Ling's mouths and more rope was used to keep the rags in place to gag them. The man Kayla had hurt managed to get up off the floor but his knee looked pretty bad. He looked directly at Ling and said something to her in Chinese. Kayla braced herself as she figured from his demeanor they were about to take a good kicking, and she was right. The gang members circled around above the girls laying tied up on the floor and started kicking them. When the gang left, Kayla and Ling were left bound and gagged, bruised and bleeding, in the middle of their wrecked dojo. Kayla was hurt, but she knew from experience she was not seriously injured. She was concerned however about the large bleeding slash on Ling's forearm; it looked deep and blood was everywhere. They needed to get free and get some help for that arm. After about an hour of struggling the girls managed to free Ling's hands and they got out of the ropes that held them. As Kayla removed the rags from her mouth she immediately said,
'we need to get you to a hospital to get that arm sorted out, you need stitches.'

Kayla found the first aid kit and bandaged Ling's arm up as best she could to stop the bleeding. As she was wrapping the dressing around her arm Kayla said, 'Do you have any idea what provoked this?... What they wanted?'

Ling looked at Kayla and said, 'someone doesn't want us here, but I have no idea who.' Ling was lying and she hoped Kayla could not see her deceit in her face.

Upstairs in their living area, the boys that had dragged Ling up there with them, told her this was her warning. Her gang had seen her back in Beijing and wanted her back. He pulled Ling's head back by the hair and whispered to her, 'You know when you're jumped in, you're in for life' into her ear. Ling had been given an ultimatum, she was to meet with her gang's leader by the end of this week or face the consequences.

Chapter 19

Kayla had planned on meeting Master Harrington at the airport, but now had to ring her and tell her she was at the hospital with Ling. Hours later, when the girls got back to the dojo, Ling with her forearm stitched up and properly bandaged now, they both nearly cried when they looked at the damage, in the clear light of day, that had been done to all their hard work. The girls were standing there taking it all in when Kayla's master appeared in the doorway, 'Kayla, Ling, are you two ok?' she said.

Kayla looked over to her master, bowed, 'Oss master' and then said, 'Yes master we are fine.' remembering as she looked at her the lesson about not showing your weaknesses when you are hurt. She felt like crying, this was not how she wanted to greet her master. She had pictured herself collecting her at the airport and escorting her through the dojo doors to a large class of students. Now, as she stood in the middle of her wrecked dojo with a large bruise across her cheek and Ling's arm in bandages, she tried to remember the lessons her master had taught her.

The three women started clearing up the mess as Kayla updated Master Harrington on everything that had happened in the last three months, including what had happened last night.

Chapter 20

Ling tossed and turned all night long, not able to sleep. She didn't know what to do. If she did not go to see her gang leader the thugs sent to wreck the dojo would be back, and this time might have instructions to kill her, and maybe even Kayla. If she did go to see him he would never let her go again and she'd be back to her old life she wanted nothing to do with now. She didn't know what do to and because she had lied to Kayla about it, she had no one to talk to about her problem. In the middle of the night Ling decided she had to go talk to Xiang, the leader of her gang. She held out hope that if she explained things to him he might let her go. She couldn't risk her friend's life by not going to see him, that was too big a price.

The next day Ling excused herself while Kayla sat talking with her master. They were hatching plans to get students through the door and were excitedly talking. Ling told Kayla she was going out for a run.

As Ling sat on the bus heading back toward her old neighborhood her stomached churned. Old memories of her days in the gang and of the orphanage, that she'd tried hard to suppress for so long, came flooding back. Ling and Kayla had looked at a property close to her old neighborhood and she could kick herself now for not excusing herself from viewing that property. Someone must have spotted her when she was in the area.

Ling walked into the dimly lit bar in a back alley in her old neighborhood where her gang hung out. It was a small bar that was used exclusively by the gang. Everyone else was too scared to use it once they had moved into it. She was scared, really scared, but tried to not show it as she walked through the door. Xiang sat drinking a beer from a bottle in the back corner of the smoky room. He was surrounded by some of the members of his gang, most of whom Ling knew. Ling's entrance to the bar silenced everyone as they stopped to watch her walk across the bar toward the back, right up to Xiang and say, 'You "asked" to see me?'

Xiang reached across the round table grabbing Ling's hand, dragging Ling and her arm across the table. He laughed and said, 'I see you got my invitation then?', ripping off the bandaging and looking at the fresh stitches in the nasty, long slash down her forearm.

Ling replied, 'Ya, I got your message you bastard!'

With Xiang's grip still firmly trapping Ling's arm down across the table, he reached up with his free hand and backhanded Ling hard across the face. 'Watch your mouth bitch.' he snarled at her.

'What do you want from me Xiang?' Ling snapped back, her anger rising in her and her street bravado starting to come back to her now. Ling was a pretty girl and had been Xiang's lover before she was arrested. Because of this she had been the gang's number two before she had disappeared after her arrest.

Xiang released the grip on Ling's arm and allowed her to stand upright again. 'Do you want a hit before we continue babe?' he said throwing a sachet of heroin on the table in front of her.

Ling replied, 'No. I just want to know what it is you want.'

Xiang sat back and chuckled a little, looking at his fellow gang members now and said, 'You think you are better than us now, don't you?'

Ling, still standing firm, said, 'Look Xiang, I don't want this life anymore. I've moved on. I just want you to leave me alone.'

With a glance and nod from Xiang two gang members, by the bar's front door, closed and locked it. They now stood in front of the only exit out. Ling's fear was rising; there were at least twenty gang members in the bar she was now locked within. She had to talk her way out of this. 'Please Xiang, I'm begging you... let me go.'

Xiang continued to play it up to the others who were clearly enjoying the show and continued harassing Ling, 'Perhaps you need to remember your place bitch.' and with another glance to the guys around the table with him, Ling was grabbed by the guys on both sides of her. They pushed her down to her knees. Ling knew she couldn't take on the entire gang so did not resist and stayed down. She hoped Xiang would have his fun humiliating her and then perhaps let her go. Xiang was enjoying his little show now, and the entire bar was riveted with what has happening at his table. He pulled open the sachet of heroin on the table and spread a short line across the table.

'She needs to do a line.' Xiang said to the two guys holding Ling on her knees. As the two started forcing Ling's face toward the heroin on the table she resisted now, there was no way she was going to snort heroin again. Ling got off her knees and ran her booted foot down the shin of the guy on her left. He released her, grabbing for his leg in pain. She swept the other guy off his feet and was about to throw a kick in his face when she felt a knife pushing into her side. As she glanced around she remembered again she was outnumbered and outgunned. Ling's attack had prompted several of the gang's members to jump up from their seats. All stood now, knives at the ready, waiting to take her on. 'Ok, ok' Ling said stopping her attacks, feeling the knife point pushing into her side and seeing the small trickle of blood on her t-shirt where the sharp knife point poked into her now. The girl that had been sitting next to Xiang fondling him while all this was going on now got up and slowly walked behind Ling. She grabbed Ling's hair, close to the scalp, and pulled back hard. At the same time she twisted Ling's arm up hard behind her back until Ling screamed out in pain, her wrist and forearm feeling like both would snap if the girl pulled up any more. 'Let's kill this bitch, she's no longer one of us.' she hissed into Ling's ear while pulling Ling's head back harder with the iron grip in her hair. Ling assumed she was now Xiang's number two and didn't want Ling coming back and taking her position.

Xiang tipped his chair back on two legs, took a swig of beer from his bottle, and said, 'Let's not be hasty. She only needs some motivation I think.', shooting a look to the girl who'd suggested they kill Ling. Xiang got up from his chair and walked over to Ling. He dug in his jeans pocket and pulled out a rubber tourniquet strip. He rolled up Ling's T-shirt sleeve and tied the tourniquet tight around her free arm. As he was tying the band tight he bent over and whispered in Ling's ear, 'I forgot babe, you like to shoot up rather than snort. Don't worry; I'll take care of you.'

Ling was begging him now, 'God no, please, no Xiang.' He ignored her pleas and lit a candle on the table, placed a full spoon of heroin into the flame, and threw a needle down on the table. He said mockingly, 'You use to love this stuff babe. After a day or two you'll be begging for more.' He pulled something else out of his pocket and as he poured it into the spoon on the flame said, 'You'll like my new concoction'.

Ling managed to kick the table in front of her knocking the candle over and spilling the spoon out over the tabletop. The girl still twisting Ling's arm up behind her back pulled up hard trying to break Ling's arm.

'Ahhh', Ling yelled feeling the pain shoot up her arm, but amazingly didn't feel her arm crack. Xiang was really mad now and kicked Ling hard in the gut knocking her down to her knees again. He looked at the girl holding her and said, 'Keep her still.' as he loaded up the spoon again. The girl put her knee into Ling's back and put a knife across her throat while keeping the tight grip in her hair. Xiang laughed as he pushed the needle into Ling's arm moments later. There was little Ling could do on her knees with a knife at her throat. Tears welled up in her eyes as she looked up at Xiang and whispered to him, 'You bastard'. After a few moments, while the drugs coursed around her system, Ling's eyes glazed over and she went limp.

Xiang said, 'Put her in the back.' as he untied and snapped the rubber tourniquet off her arm.

Chapter 21

Kayla and Master Harrington were concerned when it was starting to get late and Ling had not returned from her run. Kayla knew Ling wouldn't want to be away long with their master here and so much work to do once again to clean up the dojo and living area. Kayla wondered if the gang that had attacked them the other night were laying in wait for Ling on her run. Kayla and her master went out to try to find her.

When Kayla returned to the dojo she yelled, 'Ling, are you home?' No answer. Kayla turned to her master and said, 'Something has happened to her, she wouldn't just go out like this and not tell me if she didn't plan to be back for a long time.'

Master Harrington replied, 'Yes, I agree.' with a concerned look on her face. 'Perhaps we should ring her sifu and see what he thinks we should do.' Her master said helpfully.

Kayla said, 'Yes, I thought of that, but he doesn't speak English.'

Kayla was impressed by her master once again when she replied, 'I can speak a bit of Chinese... ring him.'

As Master Harrington spoke, what sounded to Kayla like fluent Chinese down the phone, she paused and asked Kayla, 'Do you think any of the boys that attached you knew Ling?'

Kayla said, 'No', immediately but then thought and replied, 'wait a minute, we were away from each other for a few minutes when they took her upstairs... and the guy I hurt said something to Ling before they beat us up. Looking back at it now, maybe he did know her, or at least said something specific to her.'

Master Harrington asked, 'Can you recall anything he said? Even a word or two?'

Kayla thought hard, Chinese was such a difficult language to learn and speak, everything sounded the same to her still. Kayla spoke a few words she thought she recalled. Her master translated,
'warning',
'gang',
'Xiang is a name I think.'

Her master then began speaking with the sifu on the phone again and a few minutes later hung up. 'Kayla, Sifu Suxi thinks perhaps the attack may have been a warning or ultimatum or something to Ling to go see Xiang.'

'Who is Xiang?' Kayla queried.

'Apparently he is the leader of her old gang. He and Ling were lovers. Sifu Suxi thinks he probably wants her back.'

Kayla quickly replied, 'Ling would never go back to the gang.'

Her master said, 'Not willingly. But who knows what threats were made to her that night.'

Kayla put her head in her hands, 'Why didn't she tell me!'

Kayla's master got up from the table and said, 'Come, we are meeting Sifu Suxi in Ling's old neighborhood.'

On the bus on the way over Kayla queried her master, 'Master, what will we do if we find Ling's gang. They carry knives and we will be badly outnumbered. We cannot bust into their hang out and expect no one to get hurt.'

Kayla's master assured her, 'Don't worry Kayla, Sifu Suxi said he would speak to the judge in charge of Ling's case and get the police involved.'
Kayla immediately replied with worry in her voice, 'Will Ling be in trouble?'

Kayla's master replied, 'Not if she was coerced.'

Kayla could tell her master was unhappy with her once again. She had not told her of Ling's prior associations with a gang or anything Ling had confessed to Kayla. At the time, Kayla had been happy she could handle Ling's situation by herself and keep her past a secret from the rest of the WKIA. Kayla knew she was in trouble again with her master.

Chapter 22

Ling awoke in a haze. She looked over at Xiang lying beside her in bed. 'Just like old times hey babe.' he whispered to her as he stroked her long silky black hair that lay wild around her on the pillow. Ling felt like she was in a time warp; her brain was mush and the room was spinning. She wondered what was going on and what the hell he had put into the junk he was shooting her up with.

'I think it's time for another hit for you.' Xiang reached for his lighter and lit the candle on the bedside table.

Ling pulled her t-shirt back on over her head, and with a slurred voice, said, 'I gotta go.' , still not quite sure what was happening to her.

Xiang grabbed her and pulled her back into his bed, 'Come on, play nice Ling.' He stuck a full spoon of his concoction onto the flame and balanced it there. This allowed him to have another quick grope of Ling, who was mostly compliant, as long as he kept shooting her up. When the police burst in the door moments later Ling and Xiang were embracing in bed, the empty needle beside them. The police ordered them to put their hands up and get out of bed. 'Put your clothes on', the officer ordered. Ling struggled to get her legs into her jeans in the druggy haze she now found herself in. Once dressed, both Ling and Xiang had their hands cuffed behind them and were marched out of the bedroom in the back room of the bar. The bar was now full of police officers and gang members lying, face down, on the bar floor in handcuffs. 'Found these two in the back.' the officer said as they entered the room with Ling and Xiang. 'They were shooting up back there.'

Kayla, her master, and Sifu Suxi all stood outside the bar nervously awaiting what the police would find in there and praying no one would get hurt in the surprise raid on the gang's hang out. They had had to wait over a day for the police to organize the raid after the call from the judge authorizing it based on Sifu Suxi's assertions. Kayla watched the door to the bar carefully as gang members started to be marched out, one at a time, with their hands cuffed behind them. Finally, she spotted Ling, but was immediately dismayed, when she saw her in handcuffs and being treated just like the other gang members. Kayla ran over to her. She could immediately see she was on drugs.

'Kayla', Ling slurred, eyes glazed over and stumbling all over the place.

The officer with Ling said something to Kayla in Chinese as he kept a firm grip on Ling's upper arm, keeping her on her feet as she stumbled about. Kayla's master translated, 'Kayla, you have to back off and let these officers do their job.'

Kayla, clearly distressed, said to her master, 'Can you ask them why they are arresting Ling please.'

Her master turned to Sifu Suxi and discussed it with him. He went and spoke with one of the officers while Kayla watched as Ling was put into the back of a police van with the other gang members. She had to be helped she was stumbling all over the place so badly. Moments later Sifu Suxi came back and told Master Harrington what he'd found out.

Kayla's master said, 'Apparently Ling was in the back, in bed with Xiang, and they had been drinking and taking heroin together.'

Kayla immediately defended her friend, 'She would not have willing done that!'

Kayla's master said, 'Calm down Kayla, I'm sure we can sort this all out shortly.'

Chapter 23

Kayla, Master Harrington, and Sifu Suxi sat for hours and hours at the police station not knowing what was going on. Kayla paced the floor, anxious to find out what was happening to Ling. She sat down again and banged her fist on the arm of the chair in frustration. Master Harrington, sitting beside her, placed her hand on top of Kayla's fist and calmly said, 'Ling will be ok Kayla.' Kayla relaxed her fist and let the tension drain from her shoulders, exhausted with worry. Finally, an officer came out and spoke to them. Kayla was told they could not see Ling and they were to go home. Kayla's master discussed what they could do with Sifu Suxi, not liking the response from the police officer. The sifu immediately got on his cell phone and spoke at length to someone. About thirty minutes later Kayla was taken back to the cells to see her friend. She was escorted by a uniformed officer down a long smelly, noisy corridor of ironed-barred cells that were absolutely crammed to capacity with prisoners. Kayla was shocked at the conditions. She recalled Ling's description of the time she'd spent in jail before, but seeing this for herself now made her realize how truly horrible it had been for Ling. Each small cell she passed was extremely overcrowded with only a wooden bench or the floor to sit and sleep on, and only a single toilet for all the occupants. It was hot, smelly, noisy, dirty and dark back in this area of the police station. A stark contrast from the shiny, new, air-conditioned area the general public saw out front. The officer stopped outside one of the cells and pointed to a girl huddled on her small section of the cell floor with her head hung down over a bucket. The officer banged on the bars with her truncheon and yelled over the noise, 'Ling-Mae Zhao'. After retching into the bucket, the girl looked up slowly at the officer calling her name. Kayla was shocked to see it was Ling; she barely recognized her friend. Kayla had never seen anyone she'd known look so bad. Her face was distorted with pain, her entire body was shaking badly, and her head, hair, and clothes were soaking wet in sweat. Kayla called to her through the bars, 'Ling, come over here.'

Ling got up slowly, taking the bucket with her, and made her way toward Kayla at the bars, stumbling over the other women in her cell along the way. Ling crouched down at the bars, holding onto them for stability, and hung her head down looking into the bucket once again. She struggled to speak but managed to rasp, 'Kayla, Xiang forced me to take the heroin. I fought with all my might against it, but he had his whole gang.' she had to stop to throw up into the bucket again.

Kayla replied, 'The police said they found you in bed with Xiang and you'd been shooting up with him. They thought is looked consensual'

Ling looked up at her friend, dark black circles around her glazed eyes, 'Kayla I swear he forced me. Once he shot me up the first time he must have taken me to bed... it's all a haze. It wasn't straight heroin he was shooting me up with, whatever the hell it was, it was knocking me right out. I was just starting to come out of it when Xiang shot me up again... and then the police burst in.'

Kayla continued to query Ling, 'Why did you go there in the first place?'

Ling replied, 'The guys that broke into the dojo the other night said if I didn't come meet with Xiang they'd kill us next time.' Ling started crying and begged her friend, 'Kayla, you have to believe me. You know I would have never done this on purpose.'

Kayla replied, sorry she'd not made it clear to Ling from the start, 'I do believe you Ling... I do.' she reassured her. 'I just wish you had told me rather than trying to handle it by yourself.'

Ling looked up at Kayla with desperation in her eyes and choked out, 'Get me out of here Kayla... I can't do this again.'

Kayla put her hand over Ling's shaking hand that clung onto the bars separating them. 'Hang on my friend; I will get you out of here as soon as I can.' She only hoped she was not offering something she could not deliver. She remembered Ling telling her how she wanted to kill herself the last time she found herself in this situation. She knew she needed to get Ling out of here quickly.

Chapter 24

It took Kayla, her master, and Sifu Suxi two days to get Ling released from jail. They had finally convinced the authorities of her innocence. The large slash down Ling's forearm, which would leave a scar on her for life, at least served to backup Kayla's and Ling's claim that the gang had attacked and threatened them the other night. Kayla also thought they had been very lucky that a few of Ling's former gang members had told the police that Ling had not been a willing participant. Everyone's versions of the events coincided and had managed to convince the authorities that Ling had been a victim rather than a willing participant. The amount of guns, drugs, and stolen merchandise ceased in the bar raid was going to send most of the gang down for a long time and Kayla breathed a huge sigh of relief when an officer came out and finally told them Ling was not being charged and would be released shortly.

Chapter 25

Ling sat cross-legged on the dojo floor with a blanket draped around her listening to Master Harrington. She still looked a mess, her eyes sunk dark and deep into her head. She was slowly starting to recover as the drugs were leaving her system. Kayla sat beside her friend in seiza, looking down at the floor and feeling about as bad as Ling looked. Master Harrington knew both girls were hurt, in different ways, and spoke to them with a gentle voice, 'Ling, you must start learning to share your problems with your sensei. It was foolish of you to go to Xiang on your own. Had you shared your problem with Sensei Kayla you may have saved yourself the pain you have been through the past few days.'

Ling quietly replied, 'Oss master.', looking down at the floor.

Master Harrington then looked at Kayla, 'Sensei Kayla, you should have shared with me Ling's past when you found out about it three month's ago. Had I known her history here in Beijing I would have sent you two elsewhere and not back here where trouble was sure to follow with her past.'

Kayla replied, 'Oss master.' For the first time, Kayla realized she was also responsible for what had happened and not blameless either. She had kept Ling's confession of her past gang activities to herself, thinking she could handle it all on her own, just like Ling had thought she could handle things on her own. The master continued, 'Sensei Freeman, who looks after our WKIA dojo in Los Angles is about to be made a master and will no longer be responsible for a single dojo. I am going to send you two over to replace him.'

Kayla hung her head down, she felt she had let her master down again and failed her. Her master could see Kayla was hurt. 'Sensei Kayla, you did not fail your assignment here in Beijing. You have secured us a dojo and made a good job of fixing up this space for us. We will send an older, more experienced sensei here to this dojo, one that the Chinese people will respect. I should have realized the people here would not accept a young sensei. This has nothing to do with you Sensei Kayla, it is a cultural issue, and I should have realized. We have all learnt a lesson here and, as you know from our training, learning a lesson can sometimes be a painful experience. But we don't forget the painful lessons do we?'

Kayla thought back to everything she had learned up in the mountains and thought her master was right. She never forgot the lessons that were the most painful to learn.

'Oss master.' both the girls answered her.

Chapter 26
Los Angeles

Kayla sat in, what was Sensei Freeman's impressive, large office. She had spent a week of handover with Sensei Freeman where he showed Kayla the ropes of running a large, successful dojo. He was gone now, and she was in charge of the dojo now. Kayla felt somewhat intimidated stepping into his shoes, so to speak. Many of Sensei Freeman's assistant instructors, who were staying on at the dojo, were much older than Kayla and some were even a higher dan grade than she was. Kayla had liked the idea of setting up a new dojo in Beijing and wasn't too happy about running someone else's, already established well-oiled operation. Everyone in the LA dojo kept telling her how much they would miss Sensei Freeman and what a great sensei he was. Kayla could not have been more different from Sensei Freeman if she tried; he was a six foot two, large framed black man in his early sixties that was larger than life. His presence exuded supreme confidence and his voice boomed across the dojo. Standing beside him Kayla, at five foot seven, and only twenty-four years old felt like a small child following her daddy around.

Ling walked into the office, bowed and said, 'Oss sensei', and then plopped down in the chair opposite the desk Kayla sat behind. Kayla looked small behind Sensei Freeman' large desk and huge leather chair that she sat curled up in. 'What's wrong?', Ling asked, reading her friend's expression and body language.

'This dojo doesn't need me.', Kayla replied honestly, 'and if one more person comes up to me and tells me how much they are going to miss Sensei Freeman I'm going to scream!'. Kayla slumped further down in Sensei Freeman's well worn leather chair.

Ling replied, 'Ya, this operation is pretty impressive.'

Kayla rolled her eyes, 'You're not supposed to agree with me!', and grinned a little at her friend. 'I want to make a difference here, but I just feel like I'm a substitute teacher. The assistant instructors could run this place without me, no problem.'

Ling piped up, 'You know, while you've been following Sensei Freeman around last week, I went out a few times and had a good look around this neighborhood. It's not a great area; there are gangs and drugs everywhere around here.' Ling paused for a minute to see what Kayla thought of what she said. As Kayla said nothing she continued, 'Do you remember we talked about starting a gang outreach program in Beijing?'

Kayla replied unhappily, 'Don't you think we've had enough of gangs... and trouble? I don't want Master Harington to have to come bail us out of trouble again here in LA.'

'Stop feeling sorry for yourself Kayla. The WKIA didn't spend a year of their time training you to sit in your office and sulk! Is your spirit that weak that after one set back you're going to pack it in and play it safe from now on?'

Kayla, who had her head down looking at the floor, now snapped her head up to look at Ling. What Ling had just said was like a punch in the gut. It was only a few months back, up in the mountains, that her master had challenged her weak spirit. Ling was right; she was feeling sorry for herself and playing it safe, just like she had done in the dojo all those months ago when training with her master. Master Harington had seen Kayla just going through the motions and not fighting with spirit, and now Kayla was repeating this mistake again. She smiled to herself, LA was the fresh new opponent she had to take on after the last tough opponent of Beijing. She had taken a bit of a beating in Beijing, but now she needed to pick herself up off the floor and deal with the next new opponent, LA. Just like her opponents in the dojo, each one had different challenges and things that must be overcome. And just as her master had taught her, she couldn't just roll into the next fight expecting to just survive it. She needed to find her zanshin, her remaining spirit, to fight the next opponent with a clear mind, confidence, and an indomitable spirit.

Ling interrupted Kayla's thoughts as she was thinking through the lesson of the indomitable spirit once again, 'Well?' she looked at her friend, 'what's it to be, are you going to play it safe or are we going to start something new here?'

Kayla smiled at her friend, 'You always did know when to kick my ass. Ya, let's start a gang outreach program here. I'll leave the day-to-day teaching to the assistant instructors and you and I can concentrate on this new program.'

Chapter 27

Kayla and Ling, dressed in jeans and t-shirts, approached a group of girls that were hanging out on a street corner just one block away from the dojo. As they approached, they were challenged by two of the gang members, 'What the hell do you want?' one got right up in Kayla's face.

'We just want to talk to you.' Kayla replied in a friendly tone. Kayla and Ling were quickly surrounded by the gang, looking intimidating and menacing circling around them like a pack of hungry animals. Kayla started, 'I am Kayla and this is Ling. We run the karate school one block over. We would like to invite you to come and train with us.'

One of the gang piped up, 'You two bitches couldn't teach us anything. We could beat the shit out of both of you - get lost before we do!'

Kayla was prepared for a response somewhat like this and said, 'Ok, if you come over to our place and any of you can beat either of us, I'll buy you all dinner... but if Ling and I win I would ask that you give it a try... deal?'

The gang was bored hanging out on the streets and thought this sounded rather amusing. Their leader piped up and said, 'Ya, we'll take that bet.'

Kayla told them a time to meet when she knew no other students would be around the dojo. She didn't want her normal karate students intimated with gang members entering the dojo.

Kayla was unsure if the girls would show or not, but she and Ling stood ready to greet the gang into the dojo late that evening, after normal karate classes had finished. Kayla briefly wondered about the wisdom of inviting a gang into the dojo with only her and Ling left in it after closing hours. This certainly wasn't playing it safe! The gang was late, but eventually sauntered into the front doors of the dojo. Kayla had a cardboard box ready and said, 'I'm going to have to ask you to leave your weapons at the door.' The gang complained about it, and nearly walked out, but eventually they started emptying their pockets. Kayla was amazed at the variety of weapons they carried, everything from guns and knives to brass knuckles and mace. It was a small arsenal! Kayla walked out into the middle of the dojo in her white karate gi and bare feet and said, 'Who wants to be first then?'

The girl who had made the claim that they could be taught nothing from them earlier that afternoon, jumped first at the chance, 'Come on bitch' the girl said stepping forward to face Kayla. Kayla thought about asking the girl to remove her boots but then figured the gang would probably balk at this and let it go. Kayla bowed to her opponent, which got laughs and jeers from the gang. Before she had finished bowing the girl made a grab for Kayla's shoulders and was going to throw a knee into her face. Kayla was ready for this however, never taking her eyes off her opponent, even when bowing. Kayla slid back and pushed the girl's arms that were grabbing for her shoulders down toward the floor with a large double hand parry. It was so strong, and the girl had come in with so much force and speed, that the simple act of the parry downward sent the girl hard to the floor, flying past Kayla and skidding across the dojo floor. Kayla turned to face her as she got up from the ground, now really pissed off, as her fellow gang members were laughing at her. She pulled something from her jacket pocket, and with a click, a blade appeared from the handle she held. Kayla thought to herself, 'I knew I should have searched them.' The girl lunged forward toward Kayla trying to plunge the knife into her stomach. Kayla easily stepped aside and got a hold of the girl's wrist and locked her in a painful wrist lock until the girl dropped the blade. Kayla kicked the blade over to Ling, who stood watching all this with amusement, knowing Kayla was in no danger. She'd seen Kayla disarm faster and stronger opponents with ease many times. Once the blade was out of the way, Kayla swept the girl to the floor and put an arm lock across her throat. 'Do you give?', she said calmly to the girl who had a panicked look in her eyes as she struggled to breathe with Kayla's arm across her throat. As Kayla waited for the girl to give in she recalled the panic of having your air cut off as she clearly recalled the day her master floored her and put an arm lock across her throat. The girl managed to get out, 'Ya'. Kayla released the lock and stood above her while the girl recovered on the floor. Kayla turned to the rest of the gang watching, still keeping an eye on her opponent on the floor, and said, 'Anyone else want to have a go?'

One of the gang members fancied taking on Ling, as Ling was smaller than Kayla. 'Let's see if this other bitch can fight', a girl stepped out challenging Ling. The gang didn't laugh this time when Ling bowed to her opponent and the girl did wait for her to take up a fighting position before attacking this time. The fight only lasted about fifteen seconds before Ling floored her with a single upper cut. The girl, gasping for air on the dojo floor, down on all fours, gave up winded.

Kayla again said, 'Anyone else want to try?'

After watching two of their toughest members go down fast, no one else wanted to challenge Kayla or Ling anymore. The gang's leader said, 'What's in this for you? Why do you want to teach us karate?'

Kayla replied, 'You girls are young. You have your entire lives ahead of you. I want to help you to find an alternative life and alternative way to live.'

The leader turned to walk away and said,
'Come on girls, let's get the hell out of here.' unimpressed by Kayla's intentions.

Ling said, 'Wait, can I at least tell you my story before you leave?'

The gang's leader had noticed Ling's tattoo when they had been out on the street earlier that day. She didn't recognize the gang, but assumed from the tat that it was a Chinese gang Ling was in, or had been in. She also gave Ling a bit of respect, seeing the large knife scar that ran down her forearm. She knew Ling was no push over and had seen some street fighting from her scars. So she cut Ling and Kayla a little slack and allowed Ling to tell them her story.

As Kayla sat listening to Ling, she was almost moved to tears when Ling, for the first time, spoke about what it felt like to be responsible for taking someone's life. Kayla had never pressed Ling with any further questions when Ling had told her, all those months ago, about killing a rival gang member to be accepted into her gang. Kayla knew then, as she was hearing and seeing now, that Ling didn't like talking about it. Ling obviously felt compelled to speak now, knowing these girls needed to hear the absolute worst of gang life. She told them about the heavy burden of guilt she carried around with her. A burden she could never shift and would take to her grave.

As Ling finished telling them how the gang life had almost ruined her life, she issued the girls an invitation to come back tomorrow and start lessons if they wanted to try to change their lives for the better.

Chapter 28

The next evening Kayla was shocked to see the gang back at the dojo door after closing. She didn't think there was a chance they'd show. She figured Ling's talk had maybe gotten to some of them. She gave them all karate gis and white belts and told them to change into them and remove their shoes and socks. Kayla and Ling taught the girls how to put the gi on correctly and tie their belts. Then they taught them the etiquette for bowing in. About thirty seconds into the etiquette lesson the first complaint arrived, 'This is crap, you said you'd teach us to fight bitch, not to sit on our fuckin' knees and bow and scrape to you.'

Kayla calmly replied, 'I told you I would teach you karate. Karate begins and ends with respect and courtesy. If you want me to teach you to fight, you first must learn this lesson.' Kayla had no intention of teaching any of them to fight until she was sure they would never use it... and that was going to take a long time. As a student of karate-do Kayla had taken a vow to only ever use her karate skills for self-defense. As a sensei, she needed to ensure those she taught karate to also adhere to this vow and would only ever use the skills she taught them to defend themselves, as a last resort.

Ling then piped up and said, 'There are rules in a dojo you must follow. If you do not follow the rules there will be consequences. If you cannot behave properly we will kick you out of this program. Now, the rule I want you to learn tonight is you do not call your sensei 'bitch' or anything other than sensei.'

The girl who had mouthed off said,
'I'll call her bitch if I want to call her bitch.'

Ling went over to the girl and said calmly,
'Apologize.'

The girl started to say 'Fuck you' but only got 'Fu...' out before Ling backhanded her across the face. When the girl lashed out at Ling she quickly found herself on the hard floor, swept off her feet.

Ling was standing above her and said,
'I told you there were consequences, now apologize to sensei.' Ling and Kayla had agreed before they started class they'd have to run this class a bit differently from a normal karate class, where students would try hard to follow etiquette and automatically respect them. They would never slap or floor a beginner student under normal circumstances, but they felt they were going to have to get the gang's respect by being hard and tough with them, until they either

complied or quit. The girl was mad, but knew Ling could easily take her, so she gave in and said, 'Sorry.', in an arrogant, disrespectful tone.

Ling, still standing above her corrected her, 'That's sorry sensei.', and the girl finally complied and said, 'Sorry sensei.'

Kayla, standing watching all this replied, 'Apology accepted.', and moved on as though nothing out of the ordinary had happened.

Although the gang members had been impressed by Kayla and Ling, they were not too impressed by their first karate class. They had expected to learn fast tricks to teach them to beat people up. Instead, however, they had been taught, for the majority of the class, how to kneel, bow, and respect the sensei and their fellow students properly. Kayla and Ling had run them through some basics, but the gang girls were unfit and found the low stances difficult. When Kayla ordered ten laps around the dojo, she had been amazed at how unfit the girls were, as they collapsed out of breath after only ten laps. Kayla wondered if any of them would be back the next night or if they would all quit on her; the first class had not gone down too well with most of them.

Chapter 29

'Leave these pajamas here; we won't be needing them again.' Slash, the leader of the gang, said to the others in the locker room as they changed back into their street clothes. 'This is bull shit. She's not going to teach us how to fight.'

'I thought it was kinda fun'. "Baby", the youngest member of the gang piped up, as she pulled her karate uniform off.

'If I want your opinion I'll tell it to you. Shut the fuck up.' Slash shut Baby down quickly. She walked over to her and hit her in the gut, 'I'll show you how to fight little girl.'

Baby whimpered a little as she held her gut, but knew better than to try to fight back. Slash was the leader of the gang because she was the toughest and no one had the guts to stand up to her. It was only because Baby was young and relatively new to the gang that she'd make the mistake of verbally questioning Slash's decision to quit the karate class.

As the gang collected their weapons from the cardboard box and left the dojo, Baby lagged behind. She looked over at Kayla as she left, stood there in her white karate gi and black belt tied around her waist, and wished she could continue the karate lessons. It had been a while since anyone had taken an interest in her and she liked this woman who had stood up to Slash and who was able to take out the gang's best fighters with easy skill and grace. She was disappointed Slash was not going to let them come back.

Chapter 30

Kayla and Ling were disappointed, but not surprised, when none of the gang turned up for their second karate lesson. Ling said to Kayla, 'I thought my story and lessons I have learnt the hard way would have motivated them to change.'

Kayla replied back to her friend, 'I remember my master tell me that some lessons cannot be taught, but must be lived to be understood. Unfortunately those girls will probably have to experience some of the horrors of gang life for themselves before they will be willing to change their ways.'

Ling agreed, 'Ya, I'm being stupid thinking a story about a tough life is going to change them. I wouldn't have listened to me either.'

Kayla replied, 'Your talk did get them through the door in the first place Ling. Maybe one day they will be back. I think some of them enjoyed it, but their leader, what did they call her, Slash, is the one calling the shots. I doubt she wants those girls to change or have anyone else but her telling them what to do and how to think.'

Chapter 31

Kayla was tired as she walked through the door of the apartment she shared with Ling, a few blocks away from the dojo. She had taught classes all day, since early morning, with two of her assistant instructors off sick this week. Ling sat watching the eleven o'clock news on TV. 'About time you got back. I was starting to wonder what happened to you.' Ling said looking up from the TV.

Kayla replied, 'I stayed after the last class to get some paperwork done; it was really starting to pile up and bug me'.

Ling interrupted Kayla who was about to continue telling her what a hard day she'd had, 'Shhh. Get over here and look at this.' Ling said looking and listening to the TV again. By the time Kayla put her stuff down and walked over to the TV the story was over.

'What?' Kayla said looking at Ling.

'They just had a story on about two local girl gangs that had a shoot out last night and it was pretty close to the dojo. The reporter was standing on San Palo street one block from the dojo. They said several girls were killed.'

Kayla replied, 'Do you think it was Slash's gang?'

'It could have been, not sure. They didn't give any details on the news. Maybe we should take a walk down the street again tomorrow and see what happened.' Ling replied.

The next evening, after classes, Kayla and Ling changed into their jeans and walked down the street to talk to Slash's gang. It had been a few weeks since the gang had walked out on the karate classes. Kayla figured Slash would not be best pleased to see her again and mentally prepared herself to try to avoid a fight with the girl. As they approached, Kayla and Ling noticed Slash and quite a few of the other gang members weren't around. In fact, there were only a handful of girls from the gang out on the street. Kayla spoke to the girls that were out there, 'We just saw the news about the shootings. Are you guys ok?'

Baby had seen Kayla and Ling approaching and was very happy to see them. She ran up to them and blurted out, 'Slash is dead! They killed her!' She looked scared and really distressed. One of the other members of the gang then informed Kayla and Ling that three of their members had been killed and most of the senior members had been arrested in the shootout the other night. Kayla could see all the girls were scared and traumatized by what had occurred and invited them to come back to the dojo for some food and a place to relax, rather than standing around on the street talking about it. The girls accepted her offer.

Kayla made everyone tea and had Ling order out for some Chinese food to be delivered to them. They sat in Kayla's office. She'd redecorated Sensei Freeman' office so it was more inviting now. The huge desk and chair that overwhelmed Kayla and took up a large portion of the office had been removed and Kayla had created a small area in front of her new, smaller, sleek slimline desk to allow her to informally chat with her instructors, students, or whomever she wanted to chat with privately. This area had a low round table and cushions around it. Kayla had become accustomed to sitting in seiza on the floor after her year in mountains and found the tatami mat floor and low table comfortable. The cushions were for her guests who were not always at ease kneeling on the floor. As the girls sat cross legged on the cushions, eating and drinking in Kayla's office, they told Kayla and Ling what had happened the other night. The girls' tough exteriors were now crumbling as they described their friends bleeding to death in the streets. Apparently Slash had been shot in the head and it was a very nasty sight the girls would never forget. Kayla and Ling just sat and listened, letting the girls vent their fears and anger. After listening to what had happened it seemed to Kayla that the girls that were sitting around her table had managed to stay alive and out of jail because they were the more junior members of the gang and had not actively participated in the shootout. Kayla decided to extend an invitation to them,
'Do you girls have somewhere to stay tonight?'

This prompted a discussion amongst them, most of the gang thought it was unsafe to go back to their hangout now. Kayla continued,
'Look, you are welcome to crash here tonight.'

The girls accepted. Ling chimed in,
'It's still early, perhaps you'd like to join Kayla and me in our training. Sometimes exercise is a good way to clear your head and forget your troubles for a while.'

The girls accepted, grateful anyone was willing to help them and look after them for a while.

Kayla and Ling had no trouble with these five girls this time. The girls listened to what they were told and tried their best. As Kayla was teaching the class, she was wondering what would happen when the more senior members of the gang were released from jail however. She wondered if they would try for retribution against the gang that had killed Slash and their other members. As she taught the karate, she wondered how she could stop further violence from occurring. Remembering her master's advice in Beijing about not trying to handle everything herself she decided two things, one, she would ring Master Harrington and tell her what was happening, and two, she'd go down and speak with the police tomorrow. As they bowed out of karate class Kayla was pleased to see the five gang members show proper respect and etiquette and wondered if maybe she might win some of these girls back from the streets.

Chapter 32

Kayla and Ling sat in a small interview room with a plain clothes police officer dressed in jeans and a t-shirt with his badge on a chain around his neck. He introduced himself, 'Hi, I'm Andrew O'Brien, I am a detective in our gang unit here. How can I help you two?' Kayla admired his fit body and arm muscles that bulged through his t-shirt when he reached over and shook her hand. He had brown hair, shaved very short, and a strong jaw line. He looked to be in his late twenties or early thirties Kayla thought. If it wasn't for the fact he needed a shave, he would have looked like he stepped off a marine recruitment poster. Kayla's thoughts trailed off for a moment while she thought about how long it had been since she's had time to date anyone. Andrew was clearly her type and her mind wandered. She finally pulled herself together and got her mind back on track to answer his question, when she realized he was staring at her, waiting for her to answer. 'We run a karate school very close to the gang shootout the other night and are interested to know what's happening with the gang members you arrested in connection with it.' Kayla finally replied.

Andrew smiled and said, 'You'll have to be a bit more specific. Do you know how many gang shootings we have around here?'

Kayla thought, 'Wow, perfect teeth too' as she admired Andrew. She realized she hadn't actually taken in what he said and, slightly embarrassed, had to ask him to repeat himself. Kayla replied, 'Ah, sorry, San Palo street; it's a girl gang, the leader of the gang has a street name of Slash.'

Andrew replied, 'Oh ya, that's the "Mamas" gang. Three of them killed the other night. Let me grab the files. I'll be back.'

Ling looked at Kayla after the detective left the room and said, 'What the hell is the matter with you?'

'What do you mean?' Kayla replied.

Ling smirked and said, 'You like this guy don't you... you're all flushed and you can barely string two sentences together.'

Kayla was embarrassed she'd been so obvious, but before she could reply, Andrew came back into the room looking at the files and saying, 'The "Mamas", Slash's gang, and the "Cruizers" have been at it for years. This latest set of shootings is in retaliation for the Mamas' leader slashing the face of the other gang's leader.'

Kayla thought to herself, 'guess that's where Slash got her street name and became leader.' Kayla piped up, 'We've been trying to start a gang outreach program at our karate school and were working with the Mamas gang. Can you tell us what will happen to the girls you arrested?'

Andrew told them that until the incident had been properly investigated the six Mama's members in jail could either be released or charged, depending on what could be proved or not. He told them it was difficult to determine who shot who at the moment and they had just arrested everyone they could get their hands on who was involved.

Kayla asked about the girls she had staying with her last night, without tipping her hand that she was now housing them. Andrew informed her that some members had gotten away from the police; however they felt they had arrested the girls involved with the real violence and the ones that got away were not involved with the shootings or deaths. Kayla was relieved to hear this. Kayla stood to leave, handed Andrew her business card, and said, 'I would really appreciate it if you could inform me when you have more information and you know what will happen to the girls you're holding.'

Andrew stood, took Kayla's card and said, 'You're a brave woman voluntarily working with these girls, but I wouldn't turn my back on any of these girls if I were you.'

Kayla smiled, which prompted Andrew to warn her again, 'I'm serious, these girls maybe young, but remember they think nothing of putting a bullet into someone.' Andrew handed Kayla his card and said, 'Call me anytime.' Kayla flushed again as she took the card.

Kayla had to endure Ling's teasing all the way back to the dojo, 'I saw you checking him out, don't deny it Kayla.' and it went on all the way back across town.

Chapter 33

'I can't do it!'

Nita, aka "Baby", yelled at Kayla. Her street name was "Baby", but Kayla always used the girl's real names when dealing with them. They were training in the dojo and Kayla was pushing her a little harder than she had the previous day. 'Can't is not an acceptable response in this dojo Nita.' Kayla replied back to her and continued, 'try again.'

Nita was Kayla's favorite student because she was so young and lacked some of the street toughness the other girls' possessed. Nita tried to act as tough as the others and swore an awful lot, attempting to show she was hard, but Kayla could see the little girl inside her still. Kayla could also see that Nita was naturally talented. She possessed speed, balance, and she had a sharp mind that caught on quickly, but she irritated Kayla with her bad attitude. Kayla was treading a fine line with these girls. If she pushed them too hard, they would leave and go back to the streets, if she was too soft they would not respect her or learn anything. When Nita plopped herself down on the dojo floor and said once again, 'I can't!', Kayla looked over at Ling who looked like she was about to go deal with Nita's bad behavior. Kayla stopped her saying, 'Take over the class please Sempai'. Kayla walked over and put her hand down to Nita on the floor and said, 'Come with me Nita.' Nita accepted Kayla's hand to help her up and walked into Kayla's office with her. 'Please, have a seat Nita.'

Nita plopped down on one of the cushions on the floor unceremoniously. Kayla made a cup of tea for both of them and then gracefully knelt down in seiza while balancing two cups of hot tea on a tray. Nita piped up, 'I don't know how you can sit like that. I can't do it. Kneeling on the floor at the beginning and end of class is killing my knees.'

Kayla replied, 'Kneeling, just like everything in karate, takes practice. My master made me kneel on the dojo floor for an hour every morning before we started our day's training and that is why I can now sit in seiza for long periods of time. It didn't just come to me. I had to practice and train my body to obey.'

Nita replied, 'Wow, I couldn't do that!'

Kayla wanted to smile at the girl, who, apparently still didn't have a clue what her sensei wanted to talk to her about, but Kayla kept a straight face, 'Yes, this is why I wanted to have a talk with you. Nita, you must start believing in yourself.'

Nita, used to talking back, immediately launched in, 'I do believe in myself!'

Kayla cut her off, 'Please listen to what I say and be quiet for a change.' Kayla paused a moment to see if Nita would comply. 'When things get hard, you cannot just quit. If you believe in yourself you would tell yourself you can do it. And if you try, and practice hard enough, you can. Since you've started training with me all I ever hear you say is "I can't". Do you think you can start telling yourself you can do things, and keep trying until you get it?' Nita nodded sheepishly. Kayla corrected her, 'That's "Oss sensei".

Nita, who had been slouching across the cushions on the floor, moved to try to kneel like Kayla and said, 'Oss sensei', back to Kayla in a respectful manner.

'I'm going to hold you to this and test you.' Kayla pushed a little.

'Oss sensei' came back loud and clear from Nita. Kayla thought, 'good, this girl is starting to respond!

Chapter 34

Kayla could see all the girls were tired. It was not difficult with these students to see when they were tired. The girls were huffing and puffing, making no attempts to hide the fact that they were tired, and had had enough. Kayla felt like pushing them a little further however. 'Yoi' she commanded, 'Kiba dachi, kamaete'. The girls all took up their horse stances, with a few audible groans being heard, but Kayla let this go. Ling's job as sempai was to help the girls get things right and keep order in the class and she chimed in, 'Lower your stances, bend those knees!'

Kayla then commanded, 'Two hundred punches, count them out loud - and they had better be good strong punches or you will start over again - hajime!'

Nita was the only student who completed all two hundred punches. Kayla praised her, 'Well done Nita. See, you can do it!' Nita smiled, proud of herself. Before her little chat with Kayla, she would have quit, especially when all the others did.

'The rest of you need to work on your spirit! You should never quit. Never give up! If you tell yourself you can do it, you can. Remember, your mind is stronger than your body. When your body starts telling you it's tired and it wants to quit, you need to overrule it with your brain and tell it to keep going. Your spirit is stronger than your mind. When your brain starts tell you you cannot do something, then you must overrule it with your spirit. Your spirit, deep within you, must tell your brain you can keep going, and then your brain will tell your muscles.' Kayla finished the class, happy that Nita, at least, seemed to be turning a corner.

Chapter 35

Kayla was in her office, tapping away at the PC doing the loads of paperwork associated with running a large dojo, when the phone rang.

'This is detective O'Brien from the LAPD.' The voice at the other end of the phone said. 'You asked me to call you if there were any developments with the Mamas' girls we are holding.'

Kayla was excited to hear Andrew's voice again, but kept her reply calm, 'Yes, thank you for ringing detective, what's happened?'

Andrew cleared his throat and continued, 'They are all being released this afternoon. We don't have enough for a case against any of them I'm afraid.'

Kayla couldn't believe it, 'But people were killed!' she interrupted him.

'Yes, well, what often happens in gang related shootings is we cannot figure out who the shooter is. There are so many people involved and all the weapons used are stolen and untraceable. These kids are smart enough now to wear gloves when they handle their weapons, and they never break their code of silence, saying nothing to the police. We very rarely ever have anyone, no matter now much pressure we put on them, point the finger at a fellow gang member. The gangs do some pretty nasty things to whistle blowers, before they turn up dead, to ensure silence. Anyway, we aren't able to conclusively determine who the shooters were, and the DA says we don't have a case.' Kayla was silent at the other end of the phone and the Andrew said, 'Are you still there Kayla?'

Kayla was immersed in her own thoughts. This was going to ruin the good work she'd started with the girls staying and training with her. 'Can't you hold them on anything?' she queried.

'I'm afraid not'. Andrew replied.

Kayla thanked Andrew and hung up, wondering what to do next. The last warning Andrew gave her before she hung up rang in her head, 'Kayla, please be careful, these girls can be very nasty and they are dangerous, never forget that.'

Kayla got up, looked into the dojo, and saw Ling and Nita at the heavy bag working on Nita's mae-geris. It was not a formal session, just Nita wanting some extra help. Ling was not much older than Nita really and Nita felt comfortable with Ling. Kayla called both of them into her office. She told them the news, the other gang members would be back on the streets this afternoon. Nita looked crushed by the news. Kayla continued, 'Nita, you can stay here with us. All you girls can. You don't have to go back to the gang.'

As Kayla was saying it however, she was remembering Ling's experience with attempting to leave her gang. She wondered if the LA gangs had the same code about leaving, and thought probably so. Kayla asked, 'Nita, do you want to continue your karate training and stay, or go back?'

Nita looked down and thought a minute before answering, 'I do want to continue training with you, but I cannot leave.'

Kayla pressed her, 'Why can't you leave?'

Nita answered exactly as expected, 'Once you're jumped in, you're in for life.'

Kayla asked, 'if you could undo it all and start again, would you?'

Nita quickly answered, 'Oss sensei.'

Kayla asked, 'Do you have any family here in LA?'

Nita shook her head and answered, 'My family are all back in Ohio. I ran away and ended up here in LA.'

Kayla said, 'We have dojos in Ohio Nita. I can get you back to Ohio, and you could start over again if you want.'

Nita started to cry, 'My family hate me. They won't take me back now.'

Kayla replied, 'Look, we can work on all this. If you can't go back to your family, I can work something out with the dojo sensei there. If you want out of the gang we can fix this.'

Nita nodded her head and said, 'Ok.' still in tears and not able to get much more out now.

Kayla found the other girls and told them the news. They were also torn about what to do. Kayla tried the same tactics on them as she had with Nita. This time however, it didn't work. The girls were tired of karate and wanted their gang back together again. They were all older than Nita, less impressionable, and had been in the gang a longer time than Nita. Kayla did not press them, as she knew nothing she could say would change their minds. She only wished she'd had more time with them. She thought a few weeks more might have turned the trick for them, but not the few short days they had. Kayla did not mention to them that Nita had decided to leave.

By the time Kayla and Ling had spoken to everyone it was late afternoon already and Kayla was feeling under pressure to get Nita to a safe location before the senior gang members were showing up looking for the others. Kayla, very clearly remembering what had happened to Ling in Beijing, did not want Nita anywhere near the gang when they returned. She gave Ling some cash and told her to get Nita over to the other side of town, and into a hotel for now. Kayla said a quick goodbye to Nita, said she'd be in touch tomorrow, and not to worry about anything. It was all good and Ling would look after her tonight.

Chapter 36

Kayla was in her office attempting, unsuccessfully, to do some paperwork when the girls came to say goodbye to her.

'Where's Baby?' Maria asked.

Kayla figured there was no point in lying now, they'd find out soon enough. 'Nita decided to continue her karate training. She's not going to go back with you.' she said matter-a-factly.

'She can't do that!' Maria shouted. It was an angry, automatic response.

Kayla replied, 'Why not?'

Maria shot back,' You know damn well why not.'

Kayla stayed calm, 'Look, she wants a new life, and I'm going to help her get it. I'll make the offer to you one more time... I'll help any of you leave if you wish.'

The girls actually appreciated what Kayla was trying to do and respected her for it. 'Look, we might be able to overlook this, but Shaz and the others will not let it go.' Maria was referring to the other members being released today, and the new leader, now that Slash was dead, Shaz.

'Well, I hope you can convince them, because Nita is gone.' Kayla replied. With that the girls left without a word of thanks to Kayla for housing, feeding, and training them.

As Kayla was locking up the dojo that evening, Ling rang on her cell phone and told her Nita was all tucked up nicely at a hotel on the other side of town. Kayla was exhausted and said, 'Thanks Ling, let's call it a day and skip our training tonight. I'm exhausted and I'm sure you are too. I'll see ya back at the apartment shortly.'

As Kayla turned, keys in one hand and her cell phone she'd just hung up in the other, she saw Shaz and the rest of the gang standing behind her. Shaz had a gun pointed at her. 'Where's Baby?' Shaz hissed.

'I don't know' Kayla replied. Shaz was too far away from her for Kayla to attempt to disarm her. Unfortunately for Kayla, the gang had a real good idea of how skilled she was at fighting and probably wouldn't get close enough to her, without a gun fixed on her, to allow Kayla to use her skills.

Shaz fished in her jacket pocket and pulled out some handcuffs and threw them on the sidewalk in front of Kayla. 'Put 'em on.'

Kayla knew as soon as she put the cuffs on she'd be in an even worse situation than she was in currently, so she attempted to talk to Shaz again, 'Come on Shaz, Nita's just a kid. Let her go.'

Shaz raised the gun in her hand and said with ice in her voice, 'I'm not gonna to ask you again.' Kayla had taught many self-defense classes over the years. She knew she should not go anywhere with an attacker or comply with being restrained. She normally advised people to run, knowing the average attacker would not shoot and would rather pick a more compliant victim. Kayla also knew however, that Shaz was no ordinary robber with a gun. She recalled Andrew's warning about how dangerous these girls were and thought she'd better not press her luck with Shaz. After all, Shaz had just gotten away with killing someone; she might not hesitate to pull the trigger again. Kayla was within point-blank range, there was little chance Shaz, experienced with guns, would miss. Kayla couldn't do anything really but obey, so she bent down and picked up the cuffs from the sidewalk. When she started to hook the second cuff onto her wrist in front of her, Shaz commanded, 'No, behind your back, and make 'em tight'. Kayla did as she was told. Before any of the gang members approached Kayla Shaz gave her a warning, 'I know you can kick the shit out of us, but if you try anything, I'll make it so you never throw another kick again.' she said as she pointed the gun down at Kayla's knee. 'Comprende'?'

Kayla said 'Yes' as calmly as she could, not showing her fears to them. Kayla looked into the faces of the girls who had stayed with her the past few evenings. The girls she'd cooked for, trained, and housed. None of them could look her in the eye. She could see they were torn about what was happening, but none of them were coming to her defense. One of Shaz's girls roughly grabbed Kayla by the arm and pulled her toward their car waiting up on the curb. Shaz opened the trunk and the girl holding Kayla's arm reached in and pulled out an empty canvas duffle bag. She pulled the heavy bag over Kayla's head and shoulder while Shaz checked the cuffs. She tightened the cuffs down as tight as she could on Kayla's wrists. Kayla was then thrown in the back of the trunk. Shaz looked down at her hooded prisoner in the truck and said, 'You think long and hard about where Baby is, cause next time I ask you about her I won't be askin' so nicely.' and she slammed the trunk closed.

Kayla wasn't particularly Closter phobic, but the duffle bag was tight around her shoulders and the heavy canvas closed in on her face, making it difficult to breathe in the blasting hot trunk. She couldn't see a thing with it over her head but she could feel the sweat dripping down her face. Kayla tried to move her hands in the cuffs, but Shaz had made them so tight they were cutting through her wrists with every small movement. She tried to breathe normally and calm herself down but it was difficult feeling restrained so tightly and knowing she was in the back of a closed car trunk being taken god knows where. Kayla wondered now how far Shaz would take this. Would Shaz kill her if she didn't tell her where Nita was? The girl had already taken it pretty far by kidnapping Kayla at gun point. If all she wanted to do was talk, she wouldn't have found it necessary to take Kayla anywhere. Kayla again thought of Andrew's warning to her about how dangerous these girls were. Kayla was getting more and more worried as she struggled against her restraints in the dark trunk.

Chapter 37

Kayla felt the car come to a stop and heard the trunk pop open. She then felt someone grab her legs and another person at her shoulders. She was hoisted out of the trunk to stand, still with the canvass bag over her head and shoulders. A hand grabbed and pulled tight the drawstring around the bottom of the canvas bag, shrinking the little light Kayla could see down to nothing and cutting her limited air even further. She forced herself not to panic as the heavy canvas pulled hot and tight into her face. As she was pulled along, she tripped and fell several times, not being able to see a thing. Her captures were enjoying her struggle; kicking her when she was down, and having fun poking and prodding her as they pulled her back to her feet via the back belt lop in her jeans and by pulling back on the canvas bag around her head. Kayla tried to ignore the taunts coming from her captures, 'Come on bitch... walk... stay on your fuckin' feet.' and tried to concentrate instead on where she was and what she could do when she could break free. She assumed they were in the girl's local neighborhood where most of them lived. She knew they hadn't driven very far and it seemed like possibly she was being taken into a house. Kayla could feel herself now being dragged down a flight of stairs... they were taking her down to a basement. As soon as she reached the bottom stair she was pushed down to her knees. The instant her knees hit the ground she felt a boot, hard in her gut. This was unlike the lighter, irritating kicks she'd felt when she'd tripped and fell over when being pushed along; this kick was meant to hurt. She'd had taken a lot of kicks in her martial arts career, but taking a blow when you didn't see it coming, and from a booted foot, was something different. 'Ahhh!', Kayla groaned and doubled over falling from her knees over onto the hard cement floor. While she lay on the floor someone came and ripped the canvas bag off of her head and pulled her back up onto her knees. Kayla felt relieved to get the hot, heavy bag off, able to breathe normally and see once again.

Shaz, still wielding the gun, stepped in front of Kayla 'Tell me where Baby is or I'm going to mess you up bad.' Shaz hissed as she pushed the gun's mussel hard up into Kayla's cheek.

Kayla was scared for her own safety now, but tried to sound calm when she replied, 'Shaz, Nita wants to start a new life, why won't you let her?'

Shaz responded with anger and wound up and hit Kayla hard across the face with the gun yelling, 'Tell me where the fuck you put her!' Kayla was struggling to maintain composure. She was really hurting now and was starting to realize Shaz was probably not going to draw the line and stop this until she got what she wanted; blood trickled from Kayla's lips and she could feel her lip and cheek swelling up quickly. She choked as she swallowed the pool of blood in her mouth from the hard blow of the heavy metal gun across her face. While Kayla caught her breath, trying to recover from the blow, she wondered if Nita had seen something she shouldn't have. Had Nita witnessed Shaz shoot and kill someone the other night? Shaz wanted Nita back too badly, Kayla thought. If that was true, there was no way Kayla could give Nita up. Who knew what Shaz might do to her if Nita had something on Shaz. Shaz didn't seem the type to leave potential witnesses to a murder out there. Kayla, pissed off at being pistol-whipped, spit the building pool of blood in her mouth out onto Shaz's boot and looked up at her defiantly. Shaz looked at the other gang members, all standing around watching this play out, and said to them, 'get her on her feet'. A girl standing next to Kayla reached down, grabbed Kayla's tightly cuffed wrists and pulled them up sharply behind her back. Kayla stood quickly as the pain shot up her arms as they were retched up hard behind her. Shaz wisely moved out of Kayla's kicking range with the gun. She pointed it down at Kayla's knee and said, 'You have ten seconds to tell me where the fuck she is or I'm going to permanently cripple you'.

Kayla was terrified at this prospect. A bullet in her knee would put an end to her martial arts career and change her life forever. Kayla briefly contemplated telling Shaz where Nita was. She tried to stall for time asking Shaz, 'What will you do to Nita if I tell you where she is?'

Shaz answered, 'We'll "persuade" her of the error of her ways... You have five seconds.' Kayla couldn't give Nita up. She didn't know what they would do to her, and she had promised the girl she'd get her out. 'Time's up!' Shaz yelled and raised the gun toward Kayla's knee again. Kayla closed her eyes as she heard the gun go off and waited for the sheering pain to rip through her knee, but she felt nothing. She opened her eyes to see Shaz dropping to the floor screaming in pain. Kayla turned to see Maria, one of the girls that had stayed with her over the past few days, holding a gun pointed at Shaz. She had shot Shaz! One of the other girls, Consuela, grabbed Shaz's gun that now lay on the floor. Shaz was screaming in pain and rolling on the floor holding her shoulder. It appeared Maria shot Shaz in the shoulder, only intending to wound her, not kill her. Maria said to Consuela, 'get the keys to the cuffs out of her pocket'. Consuela got the keys from Shaz's jacket pocket and uncuffed Kayla's hands from behind her while Marie held off Shaz's supporters with the gun. Consuela yelled, 'Let's get the hell out of here!' Kayla and the two girls who had helped her ran up the basement stairs, out the front door, jumped in the car, and floored it.

In the car Kayla said, 'I can't thank you two enough.' as she reached up to gently touch her swollen, bloody face and check she still had all her teeth.

Maria replied, 'I couldn't let Shaz blow your knee. Not after everything you tried to do for us.'

Kayla replied, 'You two can't go back to the gang now. Do you want to stay with Nita... my offer still applies to get you girls out of here and into a new life.'

The two girls agreed to take Kayla up on her offer, not having much choice now that Shaz would be after revenge.

Later that night, as Kayla sat on the sofa in her living room with a bag of ice on her badly bruised cheekbone, she wished Ling was there to talk to, but she'd left her at the hotel across town with the girls. Ling had insisted Kayla go home and take care of herself. Ling said she would stay and look after the girls. Kayla picked up the phone and dialed Andrew's cell phone. 'Hello' he answered.

'Hi, it's Kayla.' as she talked she realized her voice was badly distorted from the injuries to her face from Shaz's pistol.

'What's wrong?' Andrew sounded concerned. 'Are you in trouble Kayla?'

Kayla was in shock and was tired, she uncharacteristically started to cry. Andrew said, 'Where are you Kayla?'

Andrew was at the door to her apartment about thirty minutes later. When he saw Kayla he instinctively reached out to her and gave her a big hug. They sat down on the sofa and he held her gently in his arms. Kayla calmed herself down and told him an edited version of what had happened to her. She kept a few things from him, not wanting to get any of the girls she was helping into trouble with the police. Andrew didn't care about being a police officer at this moment; he genuinely cared for Kayla and was only concerned about her right now. Andrew spent the night looking after Kayla and over breakfast the next morning he shyly asked Kayla if she'd go out with him. Kayla had just come out from taking a shower and had been horrified to see her swollen, badly bruised and scraped face in the mirror. She thought to herself, 'this guy is special; he's looked after me all night, made breakfast, and now he wants to go out with Frankenstein!' she smiled to herself and told Andrew she'd love to but that she needed to go away for a few days first.

Chapter 38
Cleveland

Kayla hated getting dressed up, she was perfectly happy in her karate gi or sweats, but she thought she ought to make a good first impression on Nita's parents. Nita's parents had been thrilled to get her phone call from LA telling them their daughter was safe and sound and wanting to return home. Kayla had not told them much more than that over the phone. They had agreed to meet with her at their home in the suburbs of Cleveland, Ohio. Kayla thought it best that Nita not come on their first meeting, since she and her parents obviously had some issues. Kayla wanted to find out what Nita's parents were like and what their issues were, before throwing Nita back together with them, so she left Nita at the airport hotel for now.

Kayla was surprised when she drove into Nita's parents' neighborhood; it was a pleasant, clean, normal looking, suburban development. She had just assumed, incorrectly, that Nita had come from a poorer family and lived nearer the inner city or something. She should have realized all families have problems and issues, not just poor, inner-city ones. Kayla was even more surprised when Nita's mother answered the door. She was a beautiful woman, in her mid forties, Kayla guessed. She politely asked Kayla to come in. Kayla shook her hand and met Nita's father in their living room. They seemed like really nice people. Kayla wondered now, what had gone so horribly wrong in this family that Nita had run away to LA. She introduced herself, 'I'm Kayla. I run a karate school in downtown LA. As I told you on the phone, that's where I became acquainted with your daughter Nita.'

Her parents were dying to hear how their daughter was doing and started bombarding Kayla with questions. Kayla raised her hand gently and said, 'I'm sorry, I know you are full of questions, but I need to know what happened between you and your daughter - how she ended up in LA? - I promise I'll tell you everything after that.'

Nita's mother started, 'Nita was always a difficult child. Don't get me wrong, she's very clever, probably too smart. I think she was bored with school, it wasn't challenging her, so she started to get herself into trouble. We were handling it ok until she got herself into some real trouble when she got into a fight at school. She stabbed the other girl - we didn't have a clue she carried a knife!'

Kayla stopped her asking, 'How badly injured was the other girl?'

Nita's mom replied, 'Fortunately, she only had superficial wounds, but Nita was expelled from school and arrested. She spent a night in juvenile detention and then was allowed to come back and live with us until her court date. That's when she ran away.', her mother had some tears in her eyes as she was telling the story. 'We', she looked over at her husband, 'didn't handle the situation very well. We were so shocked that our daughter, my baby, was capable of such violence and had been arrested... well, we really laid into her and said some stupid things to her in the heat of the moment. She probably thinks we hate her and were going to walk away from her, I'd imagine. She didn't give us time to cool down and speak to her rationally about it before she ran away.' Her mother was really crying hard now and said, 'We love our daughter... we are not horrible monsters that she needed to run away from. We would have helped her and stood by her!'

Kayla chimed in now, 'Nita is confused. I think she may have taken whatever you said to her to heart, but I also think we can fix this. She loves you guys still, and you obviously love her, so we can fix this.'

Nita's mother burst out still sobbing, 'Can we see her please!

Kayla said, 'Yes, of course, you can see her tomorrow, but first I want to tell you what has happened with Nita since she's been away from you.' Kayla told Nita's parents everything, about the gang, about the shootings, about the gang wanting Nita back, and about the karate training Nita had started with her. When Kayla left Nita's parents she was happy. She knew the family would work this out and things would be fine eventually.

Chapter 39

Kayla entered the dojo, bowed, and waited for Sensei Groski to finish his class. She enjoyed watching other sensei teach, it always gave her new ideas. As he walked over toward her, he said questioning, 'Sensei Kayla?'

Kayla stood, bowed, and said, 'Oss Sensei Groski'.

He bowed back and said, 'Please come into my office.' Kayla had a long conversation with him about the three new students she was leaving in his care. Kayla felt confident, as she left his office, that he would keep her girls in line and would be a good influence on them. She was hopeful they could stay out of trouble with his help.

Kayla was tired now, but she had to make one more, unplanned stop today. As Nita had never told her she'd been arrested in Cleveland and was in trouble here, she thought she had better ensure Nita was not going to end up in jail when she turned up on the police radar again, being back in town. Kayla had gotten the details of Nita's arrest from her parents and now was waiting to see the officer in charge of Nita's case. It was a relatively quiet suburban station she sat waiting in. The officer came out to the waiting area and ushered Kayla into a small, clean interview room where they could talk in private. The officer was an older man that looked haggard and tired. He was dressed in an old rumpled suit that had definitely seen better days. He introduced himself, 'I'm sergeant Broll, I am Nita Gonzolas' arresting officer. You asked to see me?'

Kayla explained the situation to him and wasn't sure how he'd respond as he didn't give much away as she spoke. After Kayla had finished, he paused for a moment to think and said, 'Sounds like she may be on the path to straighten herself out, but I can't just make these charges disappear. They are on the record now. And they shouldn't just go away. These kids these days need to know they can't get away with things scott-free.' He looked down at the file in front of him, opened it up, and started fingering through Nita's records. He continued, 'She's charged with assault with a weapon, carrying and concealing a weapon, and, after she ran away, she's now also in contempt of court, as she didn't appear on her court date.'

Kayla rolled her eyes. Nothing was ever simple, and this was really going to screw up her plans for getting Nita back with her family and into training. Kayla asked, 'What does Nita need to do now to get this sorted out?'

Broll dryly replied, 'She needs to turn herself in and a juvy judge will decide what happens next.' Kayla told Broll she wanted to let Nita visit with her folks tomorrow and asked if she could turn herself in the following day. He agreed. As Kayla was leaving the room he said, 'If she doesn't turn herself in, it will be worse for her in court if she's caught, you understand?'

Kayla said unhappily, 'I understand. We'll be here.' and walked out. Kayla thought to herself as she walked out of the police station, back to her rental car, how all she ever wanted to be was a sensei for the WKIA and teach karate, but ever since she'd become a sensei she'd spent more time and effort sorting out her students' personal lives than teaching karate. She also thought, ironically, of how she'd seen the insides of way too many police stations recently!

As Kayla arrived back at the hotel late that evening and opened the door to her room, Nita, Consuela, and Maria sat watching a movie on TV. Kayla was tired and wanted nothing more than to throttle Nita for not telling her about her arrest in Cleveland, but Nita looked up at her with anticipation. She knew Kayla had been to see her parents. Kayla summoned the strength to be kind and gentle with her, even though she was angry at the moment. 'Nita, I need to speak with you alone.' she said and flicked off the TV. Consuela and Maria went back to their room and said good night. Kayla said with a smile on her face, 'Your parents are very happy you are back and want you to come home Nita.' Nita smiled broadly. After a few questions about her parents and home Kayla then had to change the subject, 'Nita, you failed to mention to me that you had been arrested here in Cleveland and were on the run from the law.'

Nita looked down at the bed they sat on, not wanting to look at Kayla now. 'I thought you wouldn't help me if you knew.' she said quietly. Kayla replied, 'I would have helped you if I knew and it would have made things easier if I had known in advance, but let's not dwell on that now. Today I went and spoke to the officer in charge of your case.'

Nita looked up, shocked Kayla had done this. She started to say something and Kayla raised her hand and said, 'Just listen to me Nita.' Nita shut up and listen to what Kayla was going to say. 'Tomorrow we are going to go and see your parents and spend the day with them, but then Monday you have to give yourself up at the police station.'

Nita started to protest but Kayla snapped at her, 'Shut up and listen Nita.' Kayla was tired, and she said this a bit more harshly than she intended, but it shut the kid up. 'Look, there has been a warrant out for your arrest since the day you didn't show up in court. You're in contempt of court now, along with the other charges against you. It looks like you are going to have to face the consequences of your actions now Nita. I tried my best to talk the officer in charge of your case out of prosecuting you. I told him you were on the right road now and this would set you back, but he said he couldn't undo the charges against you or the warrant either, now it was in the court's hands. Nita, you are going to have to be really brave and strong now and face up to this.' Kayla stopped now to see what Nita had to say.

'What's going to happen to me when I turn myself in then?' she questioned, her voice quiet and shaken now.

Kayla replied, 'I really don't know, but I promise you one thing, I will be there for you in court and try to convince the judge that you going to jail would serve no good purpose. You parents and I will stand by you Nita, but you do have to face up to your past mistakes now and pay the price.'

Chapter 40

Nita's parents, Kayla, and Nita all walked into the suburban police station together. Nita looked really scared, and Kayla couldn't blame the kid. She was only fifteen. Although she'd seen a lot of things already in her short fifteen years on earth, this didn't stop her from still being a frightened child at times. Kayla walked up to the officer at the counter and asked for Officer Broll. Broll came to the door at the side of the counter, opened it, and said, 'Come on back here with me please.'

In the back Kayla put her hand on Nita's shoulder and said to Broll, 'This is Nita Gonzolas, she is turning herself in, as you requested.' Broll was unimpressed by the fact that she'd turned herself in, or by the scared look in the kid's eyes. He just read Nita her rights, making no attempt to comfort Nita, or calm her fears about what was going to happen to her now. Kayla thought to herself, it was time for Broll to retire. He'd probably seen a lot of crap in his life as a cop, she was sure, but he'd lost his compassion somewhere along the way, or maybe he never had any? Broll looked up at the three adults with Nita and said to all of them, 'A female office will be escorting Nita over to juvenile hall and she'll see a juvenile court judge tomorrow morning.' Nita's parents asked if they could take her home now that she'd turned herself in, and the police knew where she was. Broll chuckled a little under his breath and replied a bit incredulously,
'She's got a contempt of court charge for not turning up for court. Do you really think we are going to let her out of our sight again before she sees a judge?'

Nita's mom, sick of Broll's attitude, piped up, 'She's just a kid for god sake!'

Broll dryly replied, 'A kid that carries and knife, stabs someone with it, and then doesn't turn up for court. Doesn't seem to me like you can control your own daughter Mrs. Gonzolas.'

Kayla, realizing after her chats with Broll, that they would get no where with this guy just said, 'Come on, let's go.' before Nita's mom had a chance to reply to the insult.

Broll escorted Kayla and Nita's parents out to the front and told them the details of her hearing on Tuesday and said he'd see them in court. Looking behind the officer at the counter, Kayla could see Nita with a female officer being finger printed. Nita had her eyes fixed on Kayla and her parents still. It broke Kayla's heart, and she imagined Nita's parents too, to watch Nita all alone back there, knowing she was going to spend the night in juvenile detention.

Nita's parents had retained a good lawyer when she'd first been arrested. They had phoned her again to handle Nita's case for them now. Nita's lawyer explained to Kayla and Nita's parents what would happen in court today, as they sat in the hallway outside the court waiting. 'Today is just the equivalent of an arraignment hearing. It will be pretty short. The judge will explain things to Nita and then ask her to enter a plea. The judge will then allow the prosecution to make a recommendation as to what is to be done with Nita while she awaits a trial. Then I will be allowed to speak on Nita's behalf. The judge will then decide if Nita will remain at juvenile hall until trial or if she can be released into your custody. Be prepared, the judge may ask you some questions.' she said looking at Nita's parents. Nita's mom was about to ask a question when they were called by the courtroom clerk to come into the courtroom. Nita was escorted into the courtroom from a side door by an officer of the court. Nita looked at her parents and smiled seeing them. She still looked scared, Kayla thought. The courtroom was small and much less threatening than Kayla had imagined. The judge entered, and things got started by the courtroom clerk reading the charges out loud. The judge looked at the table where Nita and her lawyer sat and said, 'How does Ms. Gonzolas plea?'

Nita's lawyer said, 'Ms. Gonzolas pleads guilty to all three charges. The judge questioned Nita to ensure she understood what pleading guilty meant. 'Do you understand?' the judge looked at Nita. Nita replied, 'Yes sir, I understand.', in a quiet and shaken voice. The judge looked over to the courtroom clerk and questioned, 'What's the next date we have open for a sentencing hearing?' The courtroom clerk clicked away at the laptop in front of her and replied, 'Two weeks, Tuesday the 21st.' Both the prosecutor and Nita's lawyer wrote the date down and nodded to the judge. The prosecutor then stood and stated, 'Ms. Gonzolas failed to appear in court the last time she was to appear before you, your honor. This, combined with the seriousness of the charges she has just plead guilty to, lead me to recommend she remain in secure, supervised detention until sentencing.'

Nita's lawyer then rebutted, 'Nita regrets her past actions and has shown she is now taking responsibility for her actions by turning herself in now and pleading guilty to the charges. She has reconciled with her parents and can live with them until sentencing. I ask she be allowed to remain at home under her parent's supervision until sentencing.' The judge looked down at the paperwork in front of him and then asked Nita's lawyer, 'You just said Ms. Gonzolas has reconciled with her parents. Where has Ms. Gonzolas been these past eight months then?'

Nita's lawyer was then forced to tell the judge that Nita had run away to LA. The judge looked at Nita now and said, 'Ms. Gonzolas, while I am pleased you have taken responsibility for your actions recently, the fact that you previously fled to LA, combined with the seriousness of the weapons assault charge lead me to agree with the prosecution. Ms. Gonzolas will remain at juvenile hall until sentencing on the 21st.' Nita's mom, sitting next to Kayla, gasp quietly.

In a small room used for lawyers to discuss cases with their clients, in the back of the court, Nita stood with tears in her eyes. Nita's parents were unhappy with the lawyer and were questioning why she had not tried harder to get Nita released to their custody. The lawyer explained to them that once a failure to appear charge was on the record it was nearly impossible to get a judge to release someone. Kayla thought it made sense, but also was not happy Nita was going to have to spend at least two weeks at a juvenile detention facility while she awaited her fate at sentencing. Kayla spoke with Nita while her parents berated the lawyer. 'Nita, you've got to be strong now. You must stay out of trouble while you are in there to get the best possible sentence. You can't look like you're still a trouble maker. I promise I will be back as a character witness for you at your sentencing hearing.'

Nita replied to Kayla, 'I'm scared. This is why I ran away in the first place; I couldn't face this.' she said as she looked down at the floor.

Kayla knew Nita looked up to Ling and replied to her, 'Ling did several months in a Beijing jail that was much worse than anything we could imagine here in America. If she could do it, you can make it through juvenile hall. Remember, never quit! Keep your head up and keep on trying to get through it and you can. And whatever you do, stay out of trouble in there. I don't want to tell the judge you've changed and you are different person now, and then find out you've been in a fight or in trouble while you were in detention. Nita, this could make the difference between you spending two weeks in there or doing several months. Do you understand?'

Nita automatically said, 'Oss sensei.' loud and clear. Her parents and the lawyer halted their conversation and looked over at Nita and Kayla surprised, but Nita's parents could see Nita really respected this young woman who was helping their daughter.

Chapter 41

Kayla exited the witness box. She had given a great character reference for Nita. The judge had asked her a few questions and Kayla thought her testimony and answers painted a pretty good picture of a young girl who wanted to change her life around for the better now. This was juvenile court and the proceedings were not as formal as an adult court, which gave Kayla a better chance to convince the judge of Nita's desire to change. After all the witnesses had spoken, the judge asked Nita to stand and asked her many questions. Nita was polite and respectful, something Kayla thought she'd learned at karate, and she answered the questions well. The judge announced they'd recess for fifteen minutes while he considered everything.

'Nita Gonzolas, please rise.' the judge stated, and Nita and her lawyer rose. Kayla held her breath while she waited for the judge's decision.

'Nita' the judge started, 'You have pleaded guilty to carrying a concealed weapon, assault with a weapon, and failure to appear. These are all serious charges. It appears however, that since you committed these crimes that you have made an attempt to turn your life around and reconcile with your family. While I applaud your efforts so far to change your life, you have not been on this road for a very long time yet. I wonder if you have the fortitude to carry on with your changes and stay out of trouble.'

Kayla cringed, this didn't sound like it was going they way she'd expected, Was the judge tired of people promising him they'd changed? Was he as hardened as Officer Broll and just wanted to see young people pay the price for their crimes? The judge continued, 'Nita Gonzolas, I am sentencing you to eighteen months at the juvenile detention centre.'

Kayla looked at Nita and saw her face drop; she looked crushed. The judge continued, 'I am going to suspend that sentence however, and put you on probation until your eighteenth birthday. If you break probation at any point during these three years, you will do your eighteen months sentence at juvenile hall. Aside from the normal probation conditions, which your probation officer will go through with you, I am attaching the following further conditions: One, you will remain living with your parents during the time you are on probation. And two, you will be expected to attend your karate classes after school, a minimum of four times a week.'

Kayla smiled broadly, the judge did the right thing, he was giving Nita a chance! The judge had obviously been impressed with the impact of the karate training on Nita, and making it a condition of her probation was brilliant Kayla thought.

Chapter 42
Northern Japan 10 years later

As Kayla walked up the mountain pass, looking up at the snow-capped peaks, she couldn't help but recall her journey up this pass a decade earlier when she was a student hoping to be selected as a WKIA sensei. This year, after a decade of service in the WKIA, she'd been selected to be a sensei at the camp. When Master Harrington called to tell Kayla she'd been selected, she told her it was a real honor to be chosen to teach at the camp. Kayla was thrilled, but after putting the phone down Kayla instantly remembered how rough the conditions were at the camp. She recalled how unbelievably cold it was up in the mountains over the winter months. This time, as a sensei, she'd have to set a good example to the students. She would have to, at least, act like the cold did not affect her! Still, Kayla was excited about going back to Japan and being part of the team of sensei that would train the students at the camp.

As all the sensei headed into the camp near dusk, Kayla felt inspired by this place once again. It was so beautiful and peaceful up in the mountains. A far cry from the noisy, polluted streets of LA, where she now called home. Kayla smiled as she explored the sensei's ryokan. It was nothing like the student accommodation. It was still a ryokan, but she had her own, much larger room which had a private bathroom with it's own cedar wood tub. She was told the people who ran the ryokan would draw a hot bath for her once a day and to let them know what time she wanted it ready. What a luxury, being able to soak in a hot tub after a hard day's training! Her room had it's own little kerosene heater also! Kayla thought to herself, nearly giggling with glee, 'I can't wait to tell Ling about this.'

Ling had left the WKIA and Kayla's LA dojo a few years ago to start her own karate school. She had grown tired of being a sempai, and was ready to do her own thing. The WKIA didn't allow students who had failed the selection process to re-apply, so Ling could never become a sensei for the WKIA, even though she was now a fourth dan. With Kayla's blessing, Ling had moved to another association and to the other side of LA to start her own, now very successful, dojo. Kayla and Ling still talked and trained together often and were still the best of friends. Kayla had seen a lot of Ling the past few months, needing to step up her training to get ready for this camp. Ling still beat her most of the time when sparring, which irritated Kayla, but the kid was quick! Well, she was hardly a kid anymore, Ling was now twenty eight and was also a mother now. She had a daughter she called Mingyu. Kayla didn't know how Ling managed to run the karate dojo and be a mother at the same time! Kayla and Andrew were Mingyu's godparents. They loved babysitting Mingyu for Ling, but Kayla was always happy when Ling collected her at the end of a long day of chasing Mingyu all over the apartment!   Kayla had been living with Andrew for several years now, since Ling had moved out of their apartment. When Kayla had got back from Cleveland, she had gone out with Andrew. Over time she found that her initial impressions of Andrew had been correct, he was a very special man. They'd been together now for nearly nine years. Ling, Mingyu, Andrew, and Kayla were all very happy and successful in LA.

At morning bow in, in the stone courtyard, Kayla looked over all the one hundred eager students facing them. She was looking for someone in particular, Nita. She spotted her and their eyes met. Nita gave Kayla a small smile before all the students bowed and were off for the morning run.   Kayla was pleasantly surprised once again about the perks of being a sensei at the camp, when the sensei went back to their ryokan, after the students started up the mountain path to the pagoda, for breakfast! Unlike the students, who only got rice and tea while standing around in the common room, the sensei had breakfast served to them in a common room that had a table and cushions to sit on. Kayla thought, gosh, if only the students knew! She mentioned this to the sensei next to her and he laughed saying he remember being pleasantly surprised the first time he was here as a sensei too.   Kayla spotted Sensei Komhara, whom she had not seen since she was a student here. He was now the chief sensei at the camp. After breakfast had finished, she walked over to him and bowed deeply, 'Oss Sensei Komhara'.

He bowed back to her 'Oss Sensei Kayla. It is good to see you again.'

Kayla caught him up on herself and Ling and Sensei Komhara laughed and said, 'I never thought you two would be fast friends after your first night here at camp as students!'

Kayla replied laughing, 'Ya, and I'll never forget walking up and down those stairs that night either.'

Chapter 43

At the end of the first day, when the students had bowed out, Kayla approached Nita. Nita immediately bowed and said, 'Oss Sensei'.

'Oss Nita.' Kayla replied, 'Come, walk with me down to the stream and sit a moment with me.'
Sitting down beside the stream Nita said, 'Sensei, it is so good to see you! Thank you so much for recommending me for this program.' Kayla watched the young woman sitting beside her and was proud. Nita had made it through her three year probation without any problems. Consuela, Maria, and Nita all had stayed with Sensei Groski and achieved their Shodan grades. Nita was now Sensei Groski's sempai at the dojo and had just been promoted to her Nidan grade after nearly ten years of karate training.

Kayla replied, 'You need not thank me Nita, you have earned your spot here at the camp. Sensei Groski tells me you are a fantastic sempai, and that you are helping him with some of his more difficult students.'

Nita replied, 'Yes, I try to do what you and Ling did for me when I can. It's so hard, most people don't want to listen to good advice!'

Kayla smiled, knowing only too well, after trying to help many troubled people over the years, 'Yes, I know. You can only help someone who is ready to be helped. It's difficult, but you have to sometimes watch the others, who don't want your help, self destruct.' Kayla paused and sighed,
'I visit Shaz in prison every once in a while. She's doing a life sentence now for killing someone. I tried very hard to save her from herself, but she didn't want my help. It's heartbreaking watching people throw their lives away.'

Nita could now relate to Kayla's sentiments and also thought to herself about how very different her life would have been if she had not accepted Kayla help all those years ago.

Kayla smiled at her student, 'Nita, do you remember the very first lesson I ever taught you. When you were staying at my dojo in LA?'

Nita said, 'Oss Sensei. You taught me to believe in myself and never say I can't do something… to always keep trying'.

Kayla replied, 'Yes, very good. Now, you must remember this lesson well while you are here Nita. This program will test you, like you have never been tested before. Believe me, there will be times when you will want to quit, and you will question yourself, as to whether you can do it. Remember and learn the lesson well and you can succeed.'

Nita bowed and said 'Oss Sensei, I will try my best.'

Kayla wanted to ensure Nita understood the message and continued, 'Nita... mind, body, and spirit must come together as one to become a great martial artist. The sensei and masters at this camp will forge your mind and body with the training you'll receive, but you must find your inner spirit, deep within you, and bring it into harmony with your body and mind. Your masters cannot do this for you Nita. If you can bring your mind, body, and spirit together as one, you will become and unstoppable force. This is the lesson of the indomitable spirit.'

Kayla continued, 'Nita, I also want you to know the sensei declare, before the program starts, which students they know and how well they know them. Karate is a small world really. Lots of sensei know lots of the students. We then also declare if we know a student too well, and do not think we can be objective in our observations of the student. I have declared that I cannot be objective when it comes to assessing you against other students. I am telling you this so you know whether you fail or succeed, it will be all down to you and not me.'

Nita smiled and said, 'I understand sensei.' and after a long pause she continued, 'Sensei, I know I've told you this on the phone, but now that we are here together, I feel the need to tell you again in person. I cannot thank you enough for what you did for me all those years ago.'

Kayla put her hand up stopping Nita, 'Nita, I'm proud of you. All you needed was a small push in the right direction and I was privileged to give it to you. Now go, put all your spirit into this endeavor.' The two women bowed to each other and parted company.

Kayla slept well that night in her warm ryokan room. She didn't know if Nita would fail or succeed at becoming a WKIA sensei, but it really didn't matter, either way, Nita would be fine now. Kayla had passed on the lesson of the indomitable spirit, both in the dojo and in life.

Glossary

Dan - Dan grade is a level of black belt. Shodan - first step black belt, Nidan second, Sandan third, etc. Most styles of karate require a minimum number of years experience and training before a person can be promoted to various levels of Dan grade.

Dojo – training hall, place where 'the way' is practiced

Dojo Kun – the morals or rules of the dojo

Gi – karate uniform

Hajime – begin

Kamaete – take up the position

Karate-do - 'the way of the empty hand'

Kata - literally means "form". Kata are detailed, choreographed patterns of movements, blocks and strikes, practiced by traditional martial artist to perfect their technique, timing, and breathing.

Kiai - vocal explosion of air associated with the focus of power

Kiba dachi – horse riding stance

Kiritsu – stand up

Kumite – sparring / fighting in the dojo

Mae-geri – front snap kick

Oss – sometimes used as a greeting and sometimes used to mean 'Yes, I understand'

Rei - bow

Seiza – kneeling position

Sensei – teacher in Japanese

Sempai - senior grade

Sifu – 'Master' in Chinese; a highly respected teacher

Tekki - Tekki literally means 'iron horse' and is a series of katas practiced by many different styles of martial arts. Sometimes also called Naihanchi in other styles.

WKIA – a fictional karate organization. Although there may be real organizations using this name, the author's indention in this book is that the WKIA is a fictional organization.

Yame – finish / stop

Yoi – ready position

Zanshin - literally means 'remaining spirit or mind'; it refers to a relaxed but alert state.

Zenkutso dachi – front stance

Lightning Source UK Ltd.
Milton Keynes UK
01 September 2010

159248UK00001B/412/P